THE CULTURAL TRADITION
AND OTHER ESSAYS

THE CULTURAL TRADITION

and Other Essays

Francis Neilson

Essay Index Reprint Series

 BOOKS FOR LIBRARIES PRESS
FREEPORT, NEW YORK

STANDARD BOOK NUMBER:

8369-1046-X

LIBRARY OF CONGRESS CATALOG CARD NUMBER:

69-18935

PRINTED IN THE UNITED STATES OF AMERICA

CONTENTS

I

The Cultural Tradition

AFTER THE FIRST WORLD WAR, THERE WERE SPASMODIC attempts to revive interest in what has been called "culture." These efforts were put forth by men who had spent the better part of their lives in academic institutions. The movement did not get far, because a fundamental change had taken place in the system of education. An era of specialization in nearly all branches of learning had been creeping in slowly since the time of the so-called Industrial Revolution.

After the middle of the last century, the minds of students were taken up chiefly with the names of Watt, Eli Whitney, Arkwright, Fulton, Stephenson, and Hargreaves. These inventors seemed gradually to supplant the memory of Plato, Aristotle, Chaucer, Shakespeare, Milton, and many classical and medieval masters whose names had been heard almost daily in the classrooms. Active life was given over to the business of learning how to make a living, and the cultural tradition of many centuries was broken. The few dissenters were voices of those crying in the intellectual wilderness of what was called progress.

Goethe in Germany, Victor Cousin in France, and Matthew Arnold in England made bold attempts to pick up the threads of cultural learning, but the strong tide flowing in the direction of mere material well-being was all against them. Moreover, incessant wars maimed each generation by taking the best of the youth for cannon fodder.

1

War seems to be the acid test of the culture of a people, and it is not at all surprising for us to learn from a well-known publicist: "One of the strangest phenomena of our scientific-mechanized civilization is the rapid decrease of the intellectual group that produced it." More startling, still, are the facts produced by Dr. Robert Cook in his book, *Human Fertility*. He says:

> In England a Royal Commission of experts in sociology and population concluded that the average intelligence quotient of the British people was declining about 2 points every generation. The same pattern exists in the United States, where the experts consider a similar decline a moral certainty. If this trend continues for less than a century England and America will be well on the way to becoming nations of nit-wits.

How anything different can be expected from the masses who seem to be gadget mad, who spend so many hours listening to the radio, watching television, and seeing the movies, is not easy to explain. Moreover, there seems to be no positive inclination to remedy these defects on the part of trustees of our institutions of learning, who for the most part are business men of great ability, but are culturally illiterate.

Now there can be no doubt in the mind of anyone who will take the trouble to read a little history that employers and laborers prospered materially and intellectually when the cultural tradition was maintained in the schools. One who is conversant with what the people of America and of England did three generations ago to make life happier for themselves suffers a pang of discouragement when he thinks of what the next two generations will be called upon to perform. Physically and spiritually no comparison can be made. After the Napoleonic Wars, the work done by the English masses in their own interest was an achievement we have no reason to hope will be emulated by the people of this generation.

In November, 1951, George Trevelyan, the famous historian, who, until recently, was the Master of Trinity College, Cambridge, gave the Presidential Address before the English Association. Among other remarks, he said: "Many readers today are unfamiliar with that part of history which consists of the names and legends of classical mythology, so largely employed in the poems of Milton, Shelley, Keats, Tennyson and Matthew Arnold."

During the past thirty years I have had many opportunities to learn, to my sorrow, that Dr. Trevelyan is perfectly right in his criticism. I could give a hundred instances, which would prove the truth of his remark. Take one. I was conversing with the son and grandson of my wife. The boy had been to a school of repute, and one of his studies in English Literature had been Shakespeare's play, *Hamlet*. I asked him which of the soliloquies he preferred. He did not know what I meant, for the word was quite foreign to him. I then asked if his teacher had explained Hamlet's references to Niobe and to Hecuba. He was completely fogged—so much, indeed, that his father and his grandmother were quite angry with me for putting such "hard" questions to the youth.

Dr. Trevelyan says:

> To me, history and literature have formed one study, one delight, woven together by a thousand crossing strands and threads. . . . Our grandfathers were brought up on the classics and the Bible. Both were history and literature closely intertwined, and therefore formed a marvelous education, a much finer education than any which is at all usual today.

The courageous attempt made by Robert M. Hutchins at the University of Chicago to institute classes for the reading of the Great Books was a step in the right direction, but too many of the faculty and the trustees showed no inclination to rally to its support. Indeed, I learned from some that it was merely a stunt and that it would not go far. These people were wrong in their estimate, for after a year or two, Hutchins had inaugurated classes to which adult men and women came to study the masterpieces of literature. Since then, the movement has spread, and courses are given in many cities throughout the country.

One of the stalwart supporters of the English cultural tradition passed away a few years ago. He was Lord (Alexander) Lindsay, formerly Master of Balliol College Oxford, who, upon his retirement, became principal of the newly formed North Staffordshire University College. The obituary in *The New York Times* stated:

> . . . Believing that English University education had become too stereotyped, he required all first-year students to take a broad course of general studies before specializing. Merely intellectual training, he maintained, produces "the clever ass." Thus he described the "class of people who do not believe anything that cannot be proved by judgment or statistics."

Who has not known "the clever ass"? The man brilliant in one department of knowledge, who has never read the Bible, Shakespeare, or turned the pages of the Oxford Book of Verse; the expert in a particular branch of science, who could not for the life of him give you definitions of fundamental economic terms, or state the relationship of Democritus to the atom bomb.

The complaint made by shrewd observers that the informed person of thirty-five or forty is a *rara avis* now seems to be justified. Novelists frequently remind us of the shallowness of social affairs and that the days of the cultural coterie are gone forever. English writers complain that the gatherings at Holland House marked the end of an epoch. Some of the French lament the absence of a Madame du Deffand and Mlle. de Lespinasse. Alas, the brilliant specialists of this pushful age would have been dumb dogs in such society.

Yet, it is strange that these men of one vocation, destitute of an avocation, do not realize that, in this generation, our masters of astronomy and physics are men of wide learning. To mention only a few, Sir Arthur Eddington, Sir James Jeans, and Max Planck were highly cultured scientists. Who can read Moszkowski's *Einstein the Searcher*, and fail to gather from it that his subject is a many-sided man?

These are examples that are ignored by the brilliant young specialists referred to by Lord Lindsay.

The president of a university told the writer that, at his social gatherings, many of the brilliant men were bored to death when the time came for conversation. Has this been the result of opening the higher schools to those whose only wish is to learn how to make a living? This is a question that is of the utmost importance, but the answer to it is not far to seek. Perhaps a course of study in the Great Books may do something to remedy the defects of university education. But it should be understood that culture is something more than a mere knowledge of the best that has been said and thought in the world, to use the phrase of Matthew Arnold.

It is more than eighty years since *Culture and Anarchy* was published. The effect that it had upon the middle classes in England was one of deep perplexity and, to some extent, indignation, particularly in Noncomformist circles. These people missed Arnold's aim entirely. He intended to remind all sects that there was much more to life than the business of striving for comfort and living in suburban villas. He said to them:

> . . . Culture, which is the study of perfection, leads us, as we in the following pages have shown, to conceive of true human perfection as a *harmonious* perfection, developing all sides of our humanity; and as a *general* perfection, developing all parts of our society.

This statement holds good today, and in our case it is one that should be taken to heart by every president of an institution of learning. Moreover, Arnold quotes

Ernest Renan concerning our future, and, to some extent, the criticism was in the nature of a prophecy:

> ... The countries which, like the United States, have created a considerable popular instruction without any serious higher instruction, will long have to expiate this fault by their intellectual mediocrity, their vulgarity of manners, their superficial spirit, their lack of general intelligence.

The desire of the people today to know something about the past is an admission that something is lacking in their education.

No one of cultural understanding imagines for a moment that a person can make of himself or herself a cultivated being merely by reading portions of the Great Books, and attending classes where questions are not permitted. This is a defect that should be remedied. The writer attended a class that had been studying Pascal's *Pensées*. After the session, a woman complained because she could not find anyone to explain to her certain passages she could not fathom. However, she had discovered in the biographical essay in the *Encyclopædia*, that Pascal was a scientist and a mathematician; and she wondered how he could be so religious. Poor woman! Presumably she would have been unable to say why she imagined a scientist could not be a religious man.

This incident is one example of the shallowness of our system of education. In all probability, she would have been amazed to learn that Newton was more deeply interested in certain passages of the Book of Daniel than he was in his scientific work.

The story raises a rather perplexing question: how could any student attending these classes be expected to understand Pascal, and particularly the *Pensées*, unless he or she had some knowledge of the man himself and his period? The hinterland of Pascal as a scientist, the environment of Port Royal, and the controversies between the Jesuits and the Jansenists are a study in themselves.

Therefore, if no questions are to be asked in the class sessions, it must be assumed that the student will find for himself the answers to those problems posed by a reading of the *Pensées*. Surely this is expecting too much.

There is another point that should be taken into consideration, and it concerns the values of elucidation while the theme is in the mind. If it had not been for the question and answer method of getting knowledge, Plato would not have been able to give us the *Dialogues*. Whether an anti-Socratic system is preferable may be left to intelligent thinkers to determine. Perhaps, as time goes on and the experience of these studies of the Great Books is widened, the teachers themselves will probably desire to plumb more deeply into the minds of the students, so that they may estimate the cultural value of the present system.

One of many thoughts of Pascal, which every specialist should consider, is as follows:

> Since we cannot be universal and know all that is to be known of everything, we ought to know a little about everything. For it is far better to know something about everything than to know all about one thing. This universality is the best. If we can have both, still better; but if we must choose, we ought to choose the former. And the world feels this and does so; for the world is often a good judge.

In our pursuit of knowledge, we should always be conscious that we are studying the thoughts and actions of men. Pascal kept this notion in mind. His opinion is worth remembering:

> What a chimera then is man! What a novelty! What a monster, what a chaos, what a contradiction, what a prodigy! Judge of all things, imbecile worm of the earth; depositary of truth, a sink of uncertainty and error; the pride and refuse of the universe!

Yet, everything should be done to encourage those who are assisting the movement by reading the Great

Books. If it does nothing more than bring to the notice of our people the history of the golden past of thought, it will have achieved something worth while. But it should be impressed upon those attending classes that they are taking only a preliminary step toward a goal that will bring infinite happiness to them as they grow older. Furthermore, it should be made clear to the student that culture is a very big word. Indeed, it is four-dimensional, and every civilization has had its own culture marked indelibly, even in the ruins that are left for us to survey. And, yet, through the Great Books, we can learn that all have the same periods of growth and decay.

We have reached a period in our history—that is, the history of Christendom—when every sane person should realize the time has come for taking soundings. It is safe to say that 90 per cent of the people of the world are living in dread. Although here we do not seem to be much concerned about the future, it is necessary to give a thought to what our position would be if further misfortune should fall upon the peoples of the Old World. The phrase, "It can't happen here," was repeated often by optimists in every civilization of the past. I daresay the cry was heard in Athens and, afterwards, in Rome. Yet, a creeping paralysis was at work undermining the foundations that culture had raised in its springtime, and finally brought the wonders of both civilizations to ruin. One of the books in the courses is Gibbon's *Decline and Fall of the Roman Empire*. And the student will find in it evidence of this paralysis, which may remind him that all is not well with us.

If he be an intelligent reader and grasp the central truth expressed by Pliny—"great estates ruined Italy"—he might be inclined to push his investigations further and compare economic, political and aesthetic developments in Egypt and Greece with what is taking place in our midst. Should he set out upon this quest, he will have begun to make a cultured person of himself. He will wish to know by what roads his progenitors have traveled to reach this point, and he will realize that, if he does not know, it will be impossible for him to learn what roads his heirs shall be obliged to tread.

The way of learning is long, and the farther the student travels along it, the farther the goal recedes. Soon after he starts upon the quest, he finds he has no particular end in view, for each day's work teaches him a truth he is ready to accept: the more he learns, the more he desires to know. The mountains of thought increase in height and bulk, as he leaves the valleys of his period, and he fronts the rise of the foothills of medieval learning. These widen and brighten the landscape and beckon him on. He does not falter, he feels no disheartening pang, for he has discovered already that there are precious stores of wisdom to be gained as the journey lengthens.

I have been asked many times by persons who have been attending the Great Books courses to suggest some supplementary work in which they would find a comprehensive view of the culture and civilization of a people. The Oxford Press has published two books, *The Legacy of Greece* and *The Legacy of Rome*, which have been read with profit by my friends. Another one of fascinating interest is *The Nemesis of Nations* by Romaine Paterson. But the work I would commend for those who are really earnest in their desire to know something about culture in the four-dimensional sense is *The Decline of the West* by Oswald Spengler.

The work is to be recommended because it is the most stimulating thought-producer that has appeared in my lifetime. It shocks one into thinking deeply. It cuts from under our feet the fictions of nearly all the ideologies that have blurred our vision of the true state of affairs. It is a provocative work, to use the term of the blurb-writer, and as we need to be "provoked" to be shifted from our smugness, young people can do no

better intellectually than to take *The Decline of the West*
and study it as they read the Great Books.

No volume written by a modern is as informative as
it is. Take, for example, the term "mankind," which
has led many of us astray. Here is what Spengler has to
say:

> "Mankind," however, has no aim, no idea, no plan, any
> more than the family of butterflies or orchids. "Mankind"
> is a zoological expression, or an empty word. But conjure
> away the phantom, break the magic circle, and at once there
> emerges an astonishing wealth of *actual* forms—the Living
> with all its immense fullness, depth and movement—hitherto
> veiled by a catchword, a dryasdust scheme, and a set of per-
> sonal "ideals." I see, in place of that empty figment of *one*
> linear history which can only be kept up by shutting one's
> eyes to the overwhelming multitude of the facts, the drama
> of *a number* of mighty Cultures, each springing with primitive
> strength from the soil of a mother-region to which it remains
> firmly bound throughout its whole life-cycle; each stamping
> its material, its mankind, in *its own* image; each having *its
> own* idea, *its own* passions, *its own* life, will and feeling, *its own*
> death. Here indeed are colours, lights, movement, that no
> intellectual eye has yet discovered. Here the Cultures, peoples,
> languages, truths, gods, landscapes bloom and age as the
> oaks and the stonepines, the blossoms, twigs and leaves—
> but there is no ageing "Mankind." Each Culture has its own
> new possibilities of self-expression which arise, ripen, decay,
> and never return . . . .

Here we find that notions of what culture is, seeded
in our minds by our system of education, differ considerably from those of Spengler. That is why I have called
it "four-dimensional," because it has depth, height,
length, and breadth.

Furthermore, we must understand that the "culture"
referred to by Spengler is something entirely different
from "civilization." The former refers to the springtime
of a people, and the latter to the autumn. Spengler
says, "The transition from culture to civilization was
accomplished for the classical world in the fourth, for
the Western in the nineteenth century."

This differentiation is somewhat startling, but if the reader have patience and steadily pursue the question, he will find light that will make the difference clear to him. Spengler continues:

> I distinguish the idea of a Culture, which is the sum total of its inner possibilities, from its sensible *phenomenon* or appearance upon the canvas of history as a fulfilled actuality. It is the relation of the soul to the living body, to its expression in the light-world perceptible to our eyes. This history of a Culture is the progressive actualizing of its possible, and the fulfillment is equivalent to the end . . . .

In this declaration we find that Spengler is dealing with the term culture in its widest sense and has reference only to the spring and summer of a people. For us there is no culture to be expressed, for we have entered upon the autumn, when civilization has reached its zenith and begins to decline. There will be no more giants in the arts, in literature, in philosophy; nor do I think that science will produce an outstanding man. It is to be recognized that the specialist, *qua* specialist, works in a particularly narrow field. Da Vinci was a painter, an inventor, a sculptor, a physiologist, to mention only a few of his attainments. Michelangelo was an architect, a painter, a sculptor, and a poet. One might go through the list of the great artists since Giotto, and tabulate, in nearly every case, several masterly activities for each one. Looking over the scene for the past two hundred years, it might be said that Goethe was the last of the cultural giants of Christendom.

When we use the term culture, we have little or no reference to the Spenglerian interpretation. Indeed, at best, it can mean only what Matthew Arnold attributed to it, and that is "to know the best that has been thought and said." The Great Books courses attempt to meet the desire of those who wish to make of themselves cultured men and women.

When I say that culture is four-dimensional, I mean that it has many different aspects. It is astonishing to learn that, no matter how far back we go in the most ancient records, a similarity of thought and action in the early stages of development can be traced. Fundamentals were alike in all regions. The depths of the philosophic mind were plumbed by Socrates and Jesus, and spiritually Akhenaton might have been a Galilean in his soaring quest for eternal justice.

In *A New Model of the Universe*, Ouspensky makes a thorough examination of the uses to which the term culture has been put since Sir James Fraser wrote *The Golden Bough*. To us, who use it so lightly, giving to it a narrow, modernistic definition, it is a shock to find the author of *Tertium Organum* carrying us over the border line laid down by Spengler and describing a barbaric form of culture which operates in civilization.

I doubt whether Ouspensky read *The Decline of the West*, although he reveals frequently ideas of culture in the springtime sense with which Spengler has made us familiar. He startles us by indicating clearly that there is a culture of barbarism that destroys civilization. Indeed, he says:

> The culture of barbarism grows simultaneously with the culture of civilization. But the important point is in that the two cannot develop on parallel lines indefinitely. The moment must inevitably arrive when the culture of barbarism arrests the development of civilization and gradually, or possibly very swiftly, completely destroys it.

Treating this problem historically, Ouspensky is in no doubt about his findings. He says: "All forms created by civilization undergo a process of change and adapt themselves to the new order of things, that is to say, subservient to barbarism." Moreover, he brings forward the notion expressed by Dr. Nicolai in *The Biology of War*, that fundamentally there is very little difference between the weapons used by the savage and those used by the civilized man:

> The savage killed his enemy with a club. Cultured man has at his disposal every sort of technical appliance, explo-

sives of terrible power, electricity, aeroplanes, submarines, poisonous gases, and so on. All these means and contrivances for destruction and extermination are nothing but evolved forms of the club. And they differ from it only in the power of their action. The culture of the means of destruction and the culture of the means and methods of violence are the culture of barbarism.

This must have been written before the First World War, for there are two introductions to the book: one is dated 1912, and the other 1914. Those who are not familiar with this work and *Tertium Organum* should study them and learn more about culture and civilization than can be gathered from a reading of the Great Books.

So many problems which the Great Books do not deal with are brought daily to the notice of the citizen that it is necessary for the cultured man to explore in other works for information that will enable him to gain a better notion of those matters with which he has to contend and which cause him the gravest anxiety.

I have already referred to the impasse that has been reached by the physicists and the astonishing change that has taken place since the mechanistic system has fallen into disrepute. We can scarcely pick up a newspaper or a magazine without finding an article which refers to Communism as if it were a practical system and one to be feared. Yet, we never learn from the writers of these essays what the nature of the dread system is. Probably most of the authors would be amazed at the number of varied notions about it that have been held by Socialists, Anarchists, and Fabians.

The fiercest quarrels have taken place among the mentors of the different schools of thought ever since Eduard Bernstein wrote his searching criticism of his colleague's work, *Das Kapital*. It is true that Marx's book is in the list of the great ones. Why it should be, I really do not know, because the main thesis of Marx—surplus value—was abandoned long ago by intellectual Socialists. English Fabians repudiated the theory of surplus value as far back as the time when Sidney Webb wrote *Socialism in England*.

There is a work that might be studied to advantage, which deals with this subject in a particularly fascinating way. It is *The Life of the White Ant* by Maurice Maeterlinck. This book is so important that I think it is necessary to engage the attention of the reader by quoting at some length from it:

> Their civilization [that of the termites] which is the earliest of any is the most curious, the most complex, the most intelligent, and in a sense, the most logical and best fitted to the difficulties of existence, which has ever appeared before our own on this globe. From several points of view this civilization, although fierce, sinister and often repulsive, is superior to that of the bee, of the ant, and even of man himself.
>
> In the termitary the gods of communism become insatiable Molochs. The more they are given, the more they require; and they persist in their demands until the individual is annihilated and his misery complete. This appalling tyranny is unexampled among mankind; for while with us it at least benefits the few, in the termitary no one profits.
>
> . . . A new form of fatality, perhaps the cruelest of all, the social fatality to which we ourselves are drifting, has been added to those we have met already and thought quite enough. There is no rest except in the last sleep of all: illness is not tolerated, and feebleness carries with it its own sentence of death. Communism is pushed to the limits of cannibalism and coprophagy.

I would urge all people who live in dread of what is taking place in the Soviet Union to turn to Maeterlinck's book and read it. It contains indispensable knowledge for the cultivated man.

Before I leave Spengler, I should like to suggest that young men who are taking a course in physics cannot do better than to read his chapter on "Nature-Knowledge," so that they may understand the drift toward metaphysics, which is plain to educated men. The recent pronouncements of Schrödinger, Niels Bohr, and Dirac—

to mention only a few of the great scientists—are startling.

The chapter that I recommend was written more than twenty-five years ago, and much of it is prophetic as to the direction the physicists have taken. In this respect, our elementary schools lag far behind the thought of those whose names are famous as Nobel prize-winners. Erwin Schrödinger, in his little book, *Science and Humanism, Physics in Our Time*, says: "I consider it extremely doubtful whether the happiness of the human race has been enhanced by the technical and industrial developments that followed in the wake of rapidly progressing natural science."

A revolution has taken place seemingly without the knowledge of the schools, for it is an undeniable fact that the physicists are now entering the sphere of the metaphysical, gravely disturbed at the futility of much of their work.

It is good to know there are people, interested in the development of world affairs, who pause daily for a while, wondering what is to become of their heirs. Such students of the fates of peoples as Spengler and Ouspensky are necessary to shake us out of our smug demeanor and to make us think deeply of political and scientific trends. They know there are few to meditate upon these problems, and fewer still to make effective protest against those who violate the sacred cultural tradition of Europe. Maybe it is too late for spiritual and intellectual revolt to change the conduct of affairs. What, then, can the few do to be saved—saved in the very selfish sense of living apart from the turmoil?

In our history there are many extraordinary records of those who practiced detachment, who withdrew from the historical scene and lived within cells of their own making. These were deep students who still clung to the tenets of Christian religion. They still believed the kingdom was not of this world, that they were powerless to stem the tide of soul destruction. These people lived a life of thought and were content to spend their days aloof from the fret and throb of the world, asking no more for their physical comfort than the bare means of sustenance. Yet, these were the men who preserved for us the great works of antiquity, the literary monuments of the Greeks and the Romans; they were the saviors of the pagan classics, which formed the treasures of the libraries of the monastic schools.

Perhaps it is almost impossible for a man, even of large means, to emulate these heroes of learning and retire from the busy scene. For now all are slaves of government, and toil for it whether they will or not. Therefore, it is only the few in our day who can look for respite in their declining years. The mass must keep their noses to the grindstone and survive as best they can as victims of the advertising agents of the gadget makers. There is little or no hope for them and, yet, if a revolution of the spirit were to take place, it might be possible for them to take refuge in a small room containing books that would yield the best that has been thought and said in the world.

II

Machiavelli: The Permanent Member of Parliaments

IN DISCUSSING THE PRESENT CONTROVERSY UPON THE connection between what is called Machiavellianism and the affairs of the various States at the present time, I should like to point out that it seems to me an almost useless labor to attempt to reach an understanding of the problems the Florentine politician raised, unless we go beyond the confines of our parochial notions of state-craft and view them in the light of general tendencies which affect all the nations.

We have already wasted far too much time in finding labels for this and that political difference of governing men. Since the middle of the last century, the ideas of government have changed so widely and so swiftly that it seems there is scarcely anything left of the old notions of individualism and the limits that all the chief parties of that day desired to place upon the work of the bureaucracies of the State. The so-called liberal of today is, in thought, as far removed from the Glad-stonian notion of what it was in political practice as the philosophical anarchist is from the State Socialist. Indeed, liberalism as Gladstone and Cobden defined it, is unknown as a political theory to the politicians of our time. Fifty years ago, the Liberals amongst us today would have been labeled Fabians.

Our thought has been fogged by terms that few have taken the trouble to define clearly. We have had the

17

Fascism of Mussolini; the National Socialism of Hitler; the Phalangism of Franco; the Communism of Stalin; and several other brands of State control, without much thought being given to what these really mean and what economic and political conditions existed in the various States that made it possible for these dictators—all imbued with the idea of State control—to gain power.

In our misguided search for a vague ethical theory, we have missed the essential—the determining fact, as Ranke and his pupil, Lord Acton, understood it. We have wasted time in debating moral considerations of which the subject is barren. Our parochial notions are like a concentration camp, for they keep us confined in the cell of our peculiar prejudice. Our gravest danger lies in our desire to write a history of our time that should conform to the notions we hold of a history in which man never took part.

It is not strange that there should be a revival of interest in the works of Niccolo Machiavelli. The time is ripe for a reconsideration of the counsel he addressed to Lorenzo the Magnificent. Surely we are ready to admit that we have felt and seen, since the termination of the First World War, a process of governing men that is not unlike that which is dealt with in *The Prince*. There is really nothing original in the book, famous for the alleged infamy of its contents. History supplied its author with examples of the iron law of dictatorial rule from classical times down to his own day. The work of tyrants was well known to him as it is to those of us who have observed the extraordinary changes that have taken place in the world during this generation.

The literature dealing with the books of the Florentine politician is immense. *The Prince* has been the subject of many controversies in which prelates, philosophers, politicians, and poets have taken part. During the Elizabethan period his name was as well known to the generality as that of Stalin is to us.

In the magazine, *Measure* (December, 1950), there is an article called "Immortal Machiavelli," written by Alessandro P. d'Entrèves, who is Serena Professor of Italian Studies at Oxford University. He deals with two works recently published: *The Statecraft of Machiavelli*, by H. Butterfield (London, 1940), and *Machiavelli*, by J. H. Whitfield (Oxford, 1947). Both of these authors are highly qualified to deal with the subject. As for the general survey of Machiavelli's work, they differ at many points, but as d'Entrèves says: "They maintain that it is possible to approach Machiavelli without bias or prejudice."

This seems to me the essential attitude to take, if anything is to be gained from a study of *The Prince*. Perhaps it would be worth while to take a glance at the considerations of a few of the men who have contributed essays of great significance upon Machiavelli, since the beginning of the nineteenth century. This method of approach may help to clear the atmosphere of the prejudice that his name has inspired.

After Macaulay published the essay on the author of *The Prince*, in *The Edinburgh Review* (March, 1829), there seemed to be a lull of almost a generation before students woke up to the fact that, though the Florentine had long been dead, the ideas that he expressed on government were very much alive. Yet, during this period the public interest in his methods of governing was almost nil, and it was not until the publication of the *Communist Manifesto* in 1848 that revolts in European States against autocratic governments aroused the public to the dangers of their political power. The suppression of these revolts revealed in many cases the necessity of applying the counsel Machiavelli gave to Lorenzo, not only for quelling disturbances, but for dealing ruthlessly with political opponents.

Although the day had gone when assassins were employed for the purpose of ridding a ruler of a dangerous rival, other means were adopted of silencing such people within the confines of the State. Geneva, Paris, and London became places of refuge for marked men.

When a semblance of calm was restored, rulers and their Parliaments realized that there was much cause for discontent among the masses, and certain measures of reform were put upon the statute books. Then came another long lull while the people of the chief States improved their condition, and Machiavelli was for some decades merely the name of an Italian villain who had lived in the bad old days. Only scholars of politics thought he was worthy of consideration, and many are the interesting pages to be found in their works published during the last half of the nineteenth century.

A few years after Bismarck appeared upon the scene, Machiavelli's name was used as an epithet to be thrown at his head. It was flung by many who could neither pronounce it correctly nor spell it, if they were asked to do so. Perhaps not one in a hundred thousand had read *The Prince.* When Burd's edition of the work was published in 1891, Lord Acton welcomed it in a remarkable essay, which will be found in the volume called *The History of Freedom.*

Whether or not readers will agree with the remarks set out in Mr. d'Entrèves' article, its appearance is as timely as Dr. Hutchins' searching comments appended to it. It is timely because we are undeniably face to face with a world condition in politics that may soon confront all of us with the very problem upon which the Florentine wrote over four hundred years ago. Then it concerned chiefly small States. Now the world's greatest ones are perplexed by it.

The problem is one of *control* of a community.

Who is to control?

How will control be secured?

What will be the severities of the penalties to be imposed upon dissentients?

. These are the features of the problem to be considered *now,* for Dr. Hutchins says, "Every child knows that it is the dominant political doctrine throughout the world."

To my mind (and I have given some thirty years of anxious thought to the question ever since I read Lord Acton's review of Burd's edition of *The Prince*), it is necessary, when we debate this matter of political control, to understand clearly what we really mean by the term State. Unless we fix upon a definition that covers the exercise of power politics—political control— we shall not reach a conclusion that will be satisfactory to the scholar. And this is a matter that can be decided only by those who have studied deeply the workings of the political machines in bureaucratic States.

There has been as much difference of opinion about the evil of the political State as there has been about the amoral counsel given by Machiavelli to Lorenzo de' Medici. The problem is no new one, however. It is as old as the State. The literature dealing with it is immense. From Plato and Mencius, all down the centuries to Oppenheimer and Cassirer of our day, the most famous of the world's philosophers have pondered this ever present problem. Put shortly, it may be announced thus: *What is the best form of government for men?*

The fundamental economists, sometimes called Georgists, have debated this subject keenly with State Socialists for nearly three-quarters of a century. In that way, they have acquired a larger conception of the width and depth of the unbridgeable gulf that lies between individualism and Socialism than any other group of thinkers. They have learned, through direct controversy and through the study of works by Socialists that the theory of Socialism can be expressed in the following proposals and conceptions:

> The State shall control all the means of production, distribution and exchange, for the equal benefit of all, and the State shall have power over persons, their faculties and possessions.

Theoretically, this was accepted for many years by State Socialists as a fair statement of their claims.

On the other hand, the individual asked for equal economic rights, as dealt with by John Locke in his two treatises, *Of Civil Government*. One hundred years ago Herbert Spencer made a similar demand in the first edition of *Social Statics*. Briefly, these were the two ideals which caused much bitter controversy before the World Wars took place. They were political issues that affected many Parliaments, and, indeed, brought about revolutions in Europe. Power politics, as we understand the phrase today, however, was scarcely known then to the men who ruled European States. Nevertheless, the economic problem in all of them was chiefly a domestic one, for discontent arose from the unequal distribution of wealth and the restraints imposed upon the producers by landlords who dominated the political assemblies.

It is well for us to learn something of this history if we are to appreciate the danger of the neo-Machiavellians who are in power today. Therefore, an idea of the real meaning of the concept State is essential in this debate.

The chief issue in England during the last half of the nineteenth century was State control of all the activities of men (advocated by State Socialists) versus economic right (demanded by the Radical Liberal party, composed of men who feared bureaucratic control). The experience of the Tudor, Stuart, and Hanover dynasties had convinced English Radicals that a change was necessary, if the people were to regain their freedom to produce for their own needs.

It is here, in this very dilemma, we must purge our thought of the rosy notions of economic emancipation, freedom of speech, political liberty, as goals within the reach of the millions of producers of wealth. The aims and aspirations of the democratic zealots of the past century are now regarded as dreams of over-sanguine men. They believed "the less government the better," and that the masses would solve their own economic problems if politicians would leave them alone. Now bureaucratic control is noticeable in legislation; departments multiply year after year, increasing the rolls of parasites who batten upon the producers of wealth. Sops and doles are distributed to keep the impoverished quiet and bribe them to support the party in power. Industrial self interest now earns dividends so small that once greedy capitalists have become financial slaves of politicians. Leviathan! What could Machiavelli and Hobbes think of it if they were now in Washington or London? The State (*The Prince*) is omnipotent.

Louis XI, Cesare Borgia, Lorenzo de' Medici, Henry VIII, were they to appear, would turn green with envy on learning how modern politicians have construed the counsel of Niccolo. Surely an informed taxpayer would agree with Franz Oppenheimer who defines the State as the organization of the political means for the exploitation of the economic means.

This definition is in agreement with many announced before him, but not given so succinctly—in a crystal that can be understood by plain men. Oppenheimer's work was pronounced by Adolph Wagner, Dean of the University of Berlin, the foremost German political economist, as "the most important work of its kind ever published."

It might be asked how far we have departed from the notion of the State held by Machiavelli and how the rulers of our time differ from those who governed in Florence. In recent years we have had at least three who have revealed themselves as honor pupils in the study of the counsel given in *The Prince*. Why we should shut our eyes to this fact, no one can say, nor do the historians have the courage to point out that some of the rulers of the democracies are quite ready for matriculation in Machiavelli's school. A Third World War will, in all probability, engulf the democracies in disorders that can only be quelled by means as forcible and severe as those exercised by Stalin, Hitler, and Mussolini.

It may be admitted that *The Prince's* task was comparatively simple. He had to deal with Florentines within his realm and known enemies beyond his borders. His political world was circumscribed. And let it not be forgotten that his foes, within and without his jurisdiction, were as fully capable of using the rod of iron to maintain what they considered to be order as any other ruler of that period. Before and after Machiavelli, there were men in Venice, in England, and in France who were not above using methods that were not quite Christian to preserve the State.

Lord Acton gave a long part of his life to the consideration of this problem, for it concerned directly a higher one—that of the bond that had been forged between Church and State. It must be remembered that, although Ranke was his master in history, Döllinger was his preceptor in the interpretation of it. These men had studied the problems afresh, after years of thorough research, and they knew the history of them as no others knew it. From the days of Hildebrand to the period of papal infallibility, they gathered an abundance of evidence of the workings of the system, and their findings should help us to form a worthy opinion of their industry, and place a high value upon their pronouncements.

No historian of our time has examined these problems with such judicial impartiality and vast learning as Acton gave to them. He reminds us:

> . . . It is easier to expose errors in practical politics than to remove the ethical basis of judgments which the modern world employs in common with Machiavelli.
>
> By plausible and dangerous paths men are drawn to the doctrine of the justice of History, of judgment by results, the nursling of the nineteenth century, from which a sharp incline leads to *The Prince.* When we say that public life is not an affair of morality, that there is no available rule of

right and wrong, that men must be judged by their age, that
the code shifts with the longitude, that the wisdom which
governs the event is superior to our own, we carry obscurely
tribute to the system which bears so odious a name.

Acton's experience was ripened by direct communication with Parliament itself. In the early sixties he sat
for Carlow, and then afterwards for his home borough
of Bridgnorth. He knew intimately the ministers of
both parties. How close he was to Gladstone is revealed
in his letters to the Liberal leader's daughter. I have
often thought that it is almost impossible for the
ordinary elector to know the mysterious workings of
the parliamentary machine; all of those secret desires
for preferment, influence, and emolument, that actuate
members to vote for measures which they know or feel
are mere legislative sops to pacify the ignorant.

It might be said that Machiavelli is a permanently
elected representative in every Parliament. His seat is
secure, and he has not to bother about the suffrage.
Utopian ideals may be advocated from the platforms
during an election, but if anybody labors under the
delusion that, when it is over and a new government is
formed, legislation will be introduced to redress grievance and right wrongs, all he has to do to clear his mind
of such a notion is to compare the election platforms
and pledges of the parties with the measures that are
enacted. He will find that the promised land of reform
now lies farther away than it did one hundred years ago.

What has become of the great demand for economic
liberty? Let us turn once more to Acton, who says:

> . . . The immediate purpose with which Italians and Germans
> effected the great change in the European constitution was
> unity, not liberty. They constructed, not securities, but forces.
> Machiavelli's time had come. The problems once more were
> his own: and in many forward and resolute minds the spirit
> also was his, and displayed itself in an ascending scale of
> praise. He was simply a faithful observer of facts, who
> described the fell necessity that governs narrow territories
> and unstable fortunes; he discovered the true line of progress

and the law of future society; he was a patriot, a republican, a
Liberal, but above all this, a man sagacious enough to know
that politics is an inductive science. A sublime purpose justi-
fies him, and he has been wronged by dupes and fanatics, by
irresponsible dreamers and interested hypocrites.

This was no hasty judgment. Think of the many years
of close study that prepared him to announce it. His
essay on Burd's introduction is sufficient to impress
anyone with the fact that he scoured the literature of
the past on these problems and went directly to the
original sources for the information he gathered.

In England, in 1950, I was reminded that it would be
better, in discussing the probabilities of another war, to
drop all cant and hypocrisy about morals and be prepared
to face squarely the issues at stake. The man who made
this suggestion is a famous military expert and political
student of the condition of affairs of Europe. He is no
Machiavellian. Indeed, he is what is called by those who
esteem certain English virtues a Christian gentleman. I
have always known him to be a realist, a man who
thoroughly understands that an army in which order
is not maintained will be unable to function; and it
cannot do so if order is not maintained by those who
have to produce the supplies it requires. Infractions are
to be dealt with severely, and the experiences of the
two World Wars have taught him that, for governments
to maintain themselves during a war, dissentients of a
government's policy have to be suppressed. Many,
indeed, are imprisoned without charge. Spies are shot,
and books expressing antagonistic views are put on the
political Index. All these restraints are imposed by the
peace-loving powers.

It is not necessary for any of the rulers of the democracies to study the counsel given in *The Prince* to learn
what should be done to maintain the modern State.
The good men during the wars were those who supported the government. The bad men were those who
did not. I doubt whether any of the rulers of that time

thought very much about men being conceived in sin and that the Fall put a blight upon the soul of all the descendants of Adam. Prelates, statesmen, soldiers, sailors, producers of wealth, writers, and artists went into the fray, believing firmly that the Christian God was on their side, and would help them to achieve a victory over the wicked foe. The consequences of such a triumph were not reckoned by them then; but now, after all the turmoil, men all over the world are possessed with the suspicions and fears that they have entered upon a worse state of affairs than those encountered in 1914 and 1939.

As Mr. d'Entrèves mentions Lord Acton's review of Burd's work, I should like to quote some of the remarks upon this matter made by the English Catholic historian. He says: "Knowledge, civilization, and morality have increased; but three centuries have borne enduring witness to his [Machiavelli's] political veracity." Not "moral veracity" but *"political* veracity."

The perplexed student might ask: Is it solely a matter of right or wrong that has to be determined by him who reads the counsel given in *The Prince?* Surely not, for the problem to be solved is how to rule in the interest of the governor. No one was more conscious of the difference between right and wrong than Machiavelli himself. That is made plain on page after page in his books, but mankind, as history reveals from Cleon to Stalin, is not capable of ruling itself, for long, with any degree of rectitude or abundance.

The history of the Jews is extant, and who knew better than Moses what laws of restraint were necessary to keep his people from religious and economic sin? His list of punishments for violations of the Code are the very pattern and example followed by dictators down to our own time. We sometimes forget the list of penalties in the curse chapter (Deuteronomy 28).

It may be maintained that the statutes of Moses were founded upon divine justice and that the laws of dicta-

tors are based upon the knowledge of what man is
prone to do. Still, it must be admitted that Moses was
quite familiar with his waywardness and backsliding
and that the severest restrictions were necessary to
remind the offender that obedience was essential if he
would save himself from himself.

In both cases—the Mosaic Code and that of the ruler
of a political State—respect for the law, whether it be
just or unjust, is exacted, and disobedience is punished
with the utmost severity. Even in the most liberal
State, the scepter of the ruler looks like gold, but when
a danger from within or without threatens the stability
of it, its enemies soon learn that the scepter is made of
iron. Is it not so in nature? Surely we understand what
happens when we violate one of her laws; she is merciless
with those who do so.

For the purist, concerned with ethics, and the idealist,
looking for Utopias, it is a mighty problem to know
how to resolve this question of the best way to govern
men. Kings ruling by divine right, by the grace of God,
in many cases have shown themselves to be far worse
rascals than the meanest of their subjects. This thought
prompted Milton to write in *Paradise Lost:*

> O shame to men! Devil with Devil damn'd
> Firm concord holds, men only disagree
> Of Creatures rational, though under hope
> Of heavenly Grace; and God proclaiming peace,
> Yet live in hatred, enmitie, and strife
> Among themselves, and levie cruel warres,
> Wasting the Earth, each other to destroy:
> As if (which might induce us to accord)
> Man had not hellish foes anow besides,
> That day and night for his destruction waite.

Lord Grey, the Reform Prime Minister of 1832, said
to Princess Lieven, "I am a great lover of morality,
public and private; but the intercourse of nations cannot
be strictly regulated by that rule."

The final paragraph of Acton's remarkable essay seems

to me to clinch the matter as to the influence of Machiavelli upon the rulers of modern States:

> . . . He [Machiavelli] is the earliest conscious and articulate
> exponent of certain living forces in the present world. Reli-
> gion, progressive enlightenment, the perpetual vigilance of
> public opinion, have not reduced his empire, or disproved
> the justice of his conception of mankind. He obtains a new
> lease of life from causes that are still prevailing, and from
> doctrines that are apparent in politics, philosophy, and
> science. Without sparing censure, or employing for compari-
> son the grosser symptoms of the age, we find him near our
> common level, and perceive that he is not a vanishing type,
> but a constant and contemporary influence. Where it is impos-
> sible to praise, to defend, or to excuse, the burden of blame
> may yet be lightened by adjustment and distribution, and
> he is more rationally intelligible when illustrated by lights
> falling not only from the century he wrote in, but from our
> own, which has seen the course of its history twenty-five
> times diverted by actual or attempted crime.

This was written about 1890, long before anybody
dreamed of two World Wars. There had been no great
conflicts since 1870, and the Liberals of Europe then
looked toward an era of peace and of moral advancement
of the masses. And let it be understood that the Liberals
then were Liberals, not Socialists. Indeed, the backbone
of Liberalism at that time in England was the strong
force of Radicals (the vigorous, intellectual opponents
of bureaucracy) who asked for equal rights, a settlement
of economic grievances which arose from poverty and
discontent. The State, then, showed not the slightest
inclination to exercise the iron power of *The Prince*.
Parliament was a free assembly, and any question of
moment that concerned the mass of the people could be
brought before the notice of ministers by a representative.

Now all is changed, and men tremble before the
threatening storm. Is it because some of our rulers have
not taken time to study mankind and what the mass is
capable of doing when passions are aroused? Are we in

any better position today than the people of Florence were in when *The Prince* was written? I doubt it.

It should not be forgotten in this controversy that Machiavelli wrote for the condition that existed in his day. He was conscious of the dangers that threatened the State, and its preservation was the sole object he had in view. He makes it clear that he was not dealing with *what ought to be done, but only with what a Prince should do to maintain his power*. He says:

> . . . And as I know that many have written on this point, I expect I shall be considered presumptuous in mentioning it again, especially as in discussing it I shall depart from the methods of other people. But, it being my intention to write a thing which shall be useful to him who apprehends it, it appears to me more appropriate to follow up the real truth of a matter than the imagination of it; for many have pictured republics and principalities which in fact have never been known or seen, because how one lives is so far distant from how one ought to live, that he who neglects what is done for what ought to be done, sooner effects his ruin than his preservation; for a man who wishes to act entirely up to his professions of virtue soon meets with what destroys him among so much that is evil.
>
> Hence it is necessary for a prince wishing to hold his own to know how to do wrong, and to make use of it or not according to necessity.

Are we in a position to say what ought to be done in this world crisis? Is it not beyond our wit, morally or politically, to make a policy that will save us from disaster? Have we left it too late? And shall we learn, if war overtakes us again, that the masses will eventually decide whether the omnipotent State is to enslave them under Machiavellian dictators of their own choice?

III

Locke on Property and
Natural Law

STRANGE AS IT MAY SEEM TO MODERN ECONOMISTS AND
sociologists, John Locke was not the first philosopher
to consider the question of what property is, to whom
it rightfully belongs, and what the care of it should be.
In his two treatises, *Of Civil Government*, he had the
advantage of replying to Sir Robert Filmer's *Patriarcha*,
which expressed the Tory mind on government by
divine right. This work aroused much controversy, for it
expressed notions similar to those dealt with by Hobbes
in *Leviathan*.

In the discussion which ensued, Locke was driven,
as he admits, to base his reply upon the order of natural
law and the records of those in the long past who had
agreed upon first principles in establishing conditions
under which men were to enjoy the sources that were
necessary for their sustenance, self-preservation, and the
security of their successors.

Sir Robert Filmer relied on Holy Writ for maintaining
his claim, as Locke puts it,

> That all government is absolute monarchy; and the ground he
> builds on is this:
> "That no man is born free."

However, in the Scriptures there is much that has
been overlooked in these controversies, which indicates
clearly that problems concerning property were deeply

31

considered by the prophets. An instructive work on the
political economy of the Bible could be written by an
economist who had a grasp of fundamentals. Take, for
example, the closing verses of the sixty-fifth chapter of
Isaiah. Here the prophet goes to the root of the problem
of poverty, which is, in its main aspects, a property
problem. There we read:

> And they shall build houses, and inhabit them; and they
> shall plant vineyards, and eat the fruit of them.
> They shall not build, and another inhabit; they shall not
> plant, and another eat: for as the days of a tree are the days
> of my people, and mine elect shall long enjoy the work of
> their hands.

In what respect does the economic condition of the
mass of the people today differ from that which is
referred to in these verses, written about 700 years
before the birth of Jesus? Surely it differs only in degree.
From my window I see several houses in the course of
construction, and it is obvious that the laborers who
are building them will not enjoy the work of their
hands; for they have no alternative but to enter the
labor market, and whatever they earn must be shared
with the government for maintaining the bureaucracy,
with or without the consent of the governed. Government in the days of Isaiah penalized the producer of
wealth, and government today carries on the same
system of exploiting the energies of the worker.

When we come to Socrates and the search for justice,
which is the main theme of Plato's *Republic*, we find the
fundamental upon which Locke established his thesis.
Socrates told his friends that justice is "a thing more
precious than many pieces of gold."

This unique philosophical anarchist of all time, when
describing the beginnings of a State, found no place for
the politician. His State was not political in theory; it
was economic. Indeed, he said:

. . . Let us begin and create in idea a state; and yet the true
creator is necessity, who is the mother of our invention.
Now the first and greatest of necessities is food, which is
the condition of life and existence. The second is a dwelling,
and the third clothing and the like.

Then he deals with the essential activities of the
community, and shows that the needs of mankind create
the housekeeping State. In the preliminary exposition
there is no such notion in the mind of Socrates as the
divine right of kings, or of the economic and political
power of other dictators over producers.

Then Socrates reasons thus:

And now let us see how our city [State] will be able to
supply this great demand. We may suppose that one man is a
husbandman, another a builder, someone else a weaver—
shall we add to them a shoemaker, or perhaps some other
purveyors to our daily wants?

In considering the treatises of Locke, it might be well
for those who are wrestling with the economic problems
that now confront every State in the world, to turn
again to Plato's *Republic* and find the fundamentals
that should guide them in their inquiries about justice
and property.

However, it must be admitted that, owing to the
contradictory notions of our instructors, it is extremely
difficult today for the student to understand that there
are fundamentals which do not change, and that these
must be realized, even in the complexities of the present
system, if justice is to be understood and the term
property, as defined by Locke, is to have any true
significance in our thought.

This, together with kindred questions, will be forced
upon us before the youth of this generation are called
upon to consider the proper relation of the State to
those who produce wealth.

In recent years many books upon Locke's treatises
have come from the pens of learned men. Surveying my

reading for the past ten years, I think I may say that I have had some fifteen or twenty works about him brought to my notice. The latest one is *John Locke's Political Philosophy*, written by J. W. Gough, a Fellow of Oriel College, Oxford. It is a most instructive essay and deals with the chief complaints of modern critics against the ideas of the philosopher of the Restoration. Surely this indicates a revival of interest, at our institutions of learning, in philosophical ideas that have been so abused since the work of Marx and Engels became current in our thought.

It may be said that only a small segment of the people would be concerned with the profound analytical criticism contained in these books. I search in vain among those who labor in the various trades, for an individual who is a studious reader. Even with men at the head of great industries, who are perplexed about industrial and fiscal problems, and extremely anxious about the future, I seldom find one who has time to devote to serious study of the problems that harass him. Still, it is an advantage for any victim of this system to know that these conditions need not be, and that they are perpetuated, generation after generation, because men will not reflect on fundamentals and learn why the problems exist and what direction should be taken to resolve them.

Therefore, now that there is a scholastic revival of interest in Locke's treatises, they should be reconsidered by our mentors and offered as a mind-cleansing process which will rid us of the encumbrances that have littered our thought these many years.

In the field of economics and government there is no more fascinating exercise than to clarify the seeming contradictions of Locke's thought. For over fifty years I have followed closely the writings of those who have attempted to do this, and in the latest work of this nature, mentioned above, the author has only partially succeeded in accomplishing it. Professor Gough fails to transmute the ore provided by Locke into the fine gold it contains.

Furthermore, there is a fuller history connected with the terms "justice" and "property" than Locke relied upon in his debate with Filmer. These two terms were better understood at the beginning of this era than they are now by many of our economists. There is a tradition in thought as sound as that to be found in the law and custom of the people themselves. Indeed, it might be said that the clearest minds of antiquity and the Christian Era have been devoted to an elucidation of what these terms really mean. Although the church might demur, when the idea is advanced that the mission of Jesus was dedicated solely to fulfilling the law of God, yet we cannot ignore the fact that, when He presented Himself to the Baptist at Jordan, Jesus said, "It becometh us to fulfill all justice." Later, He told the people assembled on the Mount, "Unless your justice abound more than that of the Scribes and Pharisees, you shall not enter the kingdom of heaven."

With Him justice was God's law, and the key that would open the doors of peace and happiness for all to enter in. Moreover, the saying of Jesus that confounds the higher critics is concerned with justice. He said, "I will utter things which have been kept secret from the foundation of the world." This secret was divine justice.

Before him, Socrates was the only one of whom we have record who got anywhere near a solution of this secret. And he defined it as: "Justice is the institution of a natural order in which a man can produce food, buildings, and clothing for himself, removing not a neighbor's landmark, not taking what is another's, nor being deprived of what is his own."

The theory of natural law springs from this comprehension of the term justice, as does the sacredness of all created things—all natural resources—from which man derives his sustenance by his labor. And so much was this the understanding of the terms justice and natural law that Jesus said, "Come ye blessed of my Father, inherit the kingdom prepared for you from the foundation of the world."

What law could be more ancient than that? And what better authority could Locke have for the theories he advanced than that of Jesus interpreting the law of the Creator?

Humbly I tried to make a definition of justice for my friends, and I formulated it so: "Justice is the law of Providence inherent in Nature."

Locke is perfectly right in determining that the land can be held for *use* only. No one can justly own that which is created, for it was meant for the children of men forever and forever. It is the source of their material well-being, and Nature itself is God's academy, in which the lessons of the conduct of life may be learned.

When we think of the great minds that have pondered this question, we are amazed at the benighted ignorance of some of our modern philosophers on this particular matter. For long years after Jesus passed away, the problem of the use of land, and the right of the laborer to his product, engaged much of the thought of the giants of reason. From the Early Fathers down to the time of Herbert Spencer and Henry George, it has been dealt with in a thousand volumes, and a few years before Locke set to work upon the treatises, Richard Hooker, in *Ecclesiastical Polity*, wrote about it.

But let us briefly consider some of the pronouncements of the Fathers of the Church. St. Cyprian said: "No man shall come into our commune who sayeth that the land may be sold. God's footstool is not property."

St. Chrysostom declared:

God gave the same earth to be cultivated by all. Since, therefore, His bounty is common, how comes it that you have so many fields and your neighbour not even a clod of earth?

Another Early Father, St. Ambrose, proclaimed: "The soil was given to the rich and poor in common. The pagans hold earth as property. They do blaspheme God."

St. Gregory the Great rebuked the Romans when he said: "They wrongfully think they are innocent who claim for themselves the common gift of God."

Clement of Alexandria held similar ideas. Perhaps it was Origen, the successor of Clement at the school of Alexandria, who gave us the most enlightening statement on the purpose for which man was created:

> God, wishing Man's intelligence to be exercised everywhere, in order that it might not remain idle and without a conception of the arts, created Man with needs, in order that sheer need might force him to invent arts for providing himself with food and providing himself with shelter. It was better for those who would not have used their intelligence in seeking after a philosophic knowledge of God that they should be badly enough off to use it in the invention of arts, rather than that they should be well enough off to leave their intelligence altogether uncultivated.

There is also St. Molua's advice to his brethren:

> Till the earth well and work hard, so that you may have a sufficiency of food and drink and clothing. For, where there is a sufficiency among the servants of God, then there will be stability, and when there is stability in service, then there will be the religious life. And the end of religious life is life eternal.

I take this from *Religion and the Rise of Western Culture*, the Gifford Lectures by Christopher Dawson, who says: "It was the disciplined and tireless labour of the monks which turned the tide of barbarism in Western Europe and brought back into cultivation the lands which had been deserted and depopulated in the age of the invasions."

All these quotations have the same economic ring, and their soundness cannot be questioned. The Early

Fathers and their associates knew the difference between
land and property. They also understood that justice
was not a law of man's making. Locke was on safe
ground when he took issue with Sir Robert Filmer.
Here is a quotation from Origen that Locke might have
taken for a text: "All things were created by the word
of God and by His wisdom, and were set in order by
His justice."

We should remember what the conditions were in the
early centuries of our era, which forced the leaders of
Christian thought to study the Old and New Testaments.
There were bitter controversies raging in many different
schools, and the attacks upon the doctrine held by the
Fathers were carried on incessantly. Through great
sorrow and years of tribulation, they maintained an
attidude of extraordinary heroism against their enemies.
Conviction of the essentiality of the fundamental truths
of Jesus was the rock upon which they stood firm,
prepared for any sacrifice of body. They were inspired
by the categorical imperative of the Nazarene: "Seek ye
first the kingdom and its justice, and all these things
shall be added unto you."

Owing to the persecutions, they thought more deeply
on, and held far wider views of, the gospel of Jesus than
most of the Christian writers who followed them. And,
yet, the question of God's justice was the one that
dominated the minds of many of the greatest of the
medieval thinkers. Bernard of Clairvaux said:

> . . . A just is better than an indulgent kindness; indeed,
> kindness without justice is not a virtue at all. Because thou
> art ungrateful for God's gracious goodness, by grace of which
> thou wast made, thou dost not fear the justice thou hast not
> learned to know, and so thou sinnest boldly, falsely promising
> thyself impunity. . . .

St. Thomas Aquinas, in *Disputed Questions*, declares:
"Justice is a constant and perpetual will to yield to each
one his right."

One of the most startling statements on justice is to
be found in the Sermons of Meister Eckhart, the famous
mystic: "The just man is so earnest for justice that, if
God Himself were not just, he would not care in the
least for God."

The reader will pardon so many quotations when he
understands that there was a tradition of thought on
the problems of divine justice and property, which
ran from pagan days all through the Christian Era,
down to the time of Locke.

In reading the treatises *Of Civil Government*, it is well
to remember that England had endured many innova-
tions of legal duress under the Tudor and Stuart dynasties. For example, indirect taxation was a novelty
in fiscal custom. Again, the first Enclosure Act of which
we have record was sanctioned in 1606-7, and the
practice of taking common land from the people—the
Hebrew prophets called it adding field to field—was
known only to those in the districts that suffered from
this process. Very few of the early enclosure acts were
made public. It may be doubted whether Locke knew
anything about this iniquitous proceeding. Anyway, it
is quite clear that he indulged in buoyant hopes of a
restoration that would re-establish and re-affirm the
law and custom of the land. In addition, the treatises
are a reply to the attacks of Filmer in his book upon
the principles that had been widely discussed at the
time of the Puritan revolution.

Caution should be observed when reading the sections
devoted to the fundamentals of government. This is not
easy for us to follow, because there were not the cum-
brous complexities and almost insurmountable impedi-
ments to be considered then in legislative affairs that
handicap our efforts today to bring about reform. The
phrase, "the consent of the governed," was used in a
very different sense from that in vogue in a franchised
democracy.

Whereas the desires of the people of our time are supposed to be expressed by their delegates to a legislature, only a comparatively small number of electors in Locke's day cast votes for their representatives. Many other peculiar differences must be taken into consideration when reading those sections in the treatises devoted to political government and its formation.

Let us now examine some of the passages in the second treatise over which so much controversy has arisen. In Chaper V, *Of Property*, we find the following statement:

> Though the earth and all inferior creatures be common to all men, yet every man has a "property" in his own "person." This nobody has any right to but himself. The "labour" of his body and the "work" of his hands, we may say, are properly his. Whatsoever, then, he removes out of the state of Nature hath provided and left it in, he hath mixed his labour with it, and joined to it something that is his own, and thereby makes it his property. It being by him removed from the common state Nature placed it in, it hath by this labour something annexed to it that excludes the common right of other men. For this "labour" being the unquestionable property of the labourer, no man but he can have a right to what that is once joined to, at least where there is enough, and as good left in common for others.

It would be impossible to say how many times I have read and reflected upon this paragraph, and wondered why it has been so often misunderstood. Perhaps one of the chief difficulties is that the men of today, who study Locke, read him with minds clogged with notions of government and law that were absolutely foreign to the thought of philosophers two hundred and fifty years ago. Rationalism, Comteism, Marxism, and several other political and social proposals have so confused the minds of many of our thinkers that they would translate Locke in the terms of current nostrums. This cannot be done. People who believe that a government should be a pawn shop in which they pledge their labor for a loaf are not capable of understanding this passage. Locke says: "Every man has a 'property' in his own 'person.' '' Some of his critics find fault with the use, in this relation, of the term "property," and consider that Locke has blundered and is guilty of a contradiction in terms by placing it there.

Now the sense in which a man can be said to have a property in himself was quite clear to many thinkers of his day. Naturally, his opponents protested against it as a liberty taken to justify his declaration. But when we consider that a man has a property in himself because he is the proprietor of himself, Locke's statement is clear. If a man is not proprietor of himself, then he is a slave. Many leading words have taken on new meanings. When we look at the root of this word, we find that it means, according to the Latin dictionary, "not common with others; one's own, proper, belonging to one's self alone."

Locke was a Latinist and knew the roots of the words he used. But since the days of Proudhon and Marx, the term "property" has lost its own significance and meaning, for it has been employed to include many legal fictions, particularly land. If a man is not the proprietor of himself, who will dare say who is? Although today we hear so much talk of a free democracy, who will deny that the landowner and the government have first claim upon the activities and the produce of labor?

We speak quite another language now, one so far removed from the thought of Locke that it is not surprising that the twentieth-century mind cannot grasp what Locke was driving at. The phrase "social justice" has completely supplanted that of economic justice in the understanding of the people.

Many of the critics of Locke's economics are so far afield from a proper comprehension of his association of these two terms, "the law of nature" and "God's justice," that I often wonder why some of those who are of the Lockian school have failed to realize the importance of these fundamentals in the thesis. It is expressed clearly enough in Chapter II of the second treatise. There we read:

> This equality of men by Nature, the judicious Hooker looks upon as so evident in itself, and beyond all question, that he makes it the foundation of that obligation to mutual love amongst men on which he builds the duties they owe one another, and from whence he derives the great maxims of justice and charity. . . .

Even in the first treatise, he makes no mistake in associating justice with property, for he says: "Justice gives every man a title to the product of his honest industry and the fair acquisitions of his ancestors descended to him." In this there is no confusing of the term property with land, the source from which man produces the necessaries of life.

Moreover, he realizes that "Government has no other end but the preservation of property." This statement should make the reader realize how far along the road of legislative iniquity we have traveled since the days of Locke. How different it must have been even at the time when Hooker wrote.

> Human laws are measures in respect of men whose actions they must direct, howbeit such measures they are as have also their higher rules to be measured by, which rules are two— the law of God and the law of Nature; so that laws human must be made according to the general laws of Nature, and without contradiction to any positive law of Scripture, otherwise they are ill made.

Both to the author of *Ecclesiastical Polity* and his famous pupil, there must have been a bright gleam of hope in the vision of many men that better days were coming for the English people than they had known since the reign of Richard II. And why not? Surely they had good reason to dream of a restoration of the rights and customs which the English people once enjoyed. When Sir John Fortescue was Chancellor to Henry VI, he wrote a book called *In Praise of the Laws of England*.

It is hard for us to imagine that there was ever such a
condition in any political State as the one that Fortescue
describes:

> Neither doth the King there, either by himself or by his
> servants and officers, levy upon his subjects tollages, subsidies,
> or any other burdens, or alter their laws or make new laws
> without the express consent and agreement of his whole
> realm in his Parliament. Wherefore every inhibiter of that
> realm useth and enjoyeth at his pleasure all the profits and
> commodities which by his own travail, or by the labour of
> others, he gaineth by land and water. . . . They have great
> store of all hustlements and implements of household. They
> are plentifully furnished with all other things that are
> requisite to the accomplishment of a quiet and wealthy life.

England has never recovered from the economic
changes that were brought about by the depopulation
of the countryside. It is all very well for the defenders
of landlords' aggressions against the common rights of
the people to make a case for the development of agriculture, and what was called the necessity of enclosing
the land, so that greater crops might be produced than
the common folk harvested; but to deprive them of their
birthright and scatter them abroad until, as Autolycus
says, "Gallows and knock are too powerful on the high-
way; beating and hanging are terrors to me" and that
for the dispossessed there was left only "a thievish
living on the common road," was a heinous crime. In
The Winter's Tale and other plays, Shakespeare gives us a
hint of the terrible conditions of the time.

All these factors should be kept in mind when the
reader studies Locke's treatises. As for the desire to
found the principles of government upon justice, man's
right to use the earth, and enjoy the goods he produces
from it, the time had come at the end of the Stuart
dynasty when it was necessary to revive an interest in
the fundamentals of government, and many of the finest
minds of that period received the work of Locke as the
old gospel restated by a philosophical genius.

It is not an anachronism to be reminded, in this connection, of the words written by Queen Anne's great statesman, the Duke of Shrewsbury, to Lord Somers. When "the finest gentleman we have" (as Jonathan Swift described him) was pressed to return to public life, he declared that if he had a son, he "would sooner bind him to a cobbler than a courtier and a hangman than a statesman." The conditions in England in which Locke passed most of his life were so iniquitous that the wonder is, in writing his treatises, he has abstained from describing them and seemingly preferred to devote his powers to the elucidation of establishing a correct form of government.

How so much misunderstanding has arisen about the way Locke has employed the terms "land" and "property" can be explained only by the confused thought of our day, tinctured so deeply by socialistic notions. To me the passages are clear enough and the distinct difference between land and property is plain. I do not think there is one in the whole of the essay in which he is not careful to employ the term "use" when he considers a producer's proprietorship in that parcel. Nowhere does he sanction the ownership of land for the purpose of exploiting the labor of others.

A tiller is proprietor of the use-purpose of the land that he occupies. And Locke has good Biblical authority for that, for Moses laid it down on the settlement of Canaan that, when the sections were distributed to the people and their lots circumscribed, boundary stones should be placed to mark off each one. The edict went forth, "Thou shalt not remove thy neighbor's landmark." This signified that the man using that plot was "proprietor" of it so long as he tilled it. Indeed, Locke was so firm in his belief of this that he wrote:

> . . . As much land as a man tills, plants, improves, cultivates, and can use the produce of, so much is his property. He by his labour does, *as it were*, enclose it from the common. Nor will

it invalidate his right to say everybody else has an equal title to it, and therefore he cannot appropriate, he cannot enclose, without the consent of all his fellow-commoners, all mankind. . . . .

There should be no difficulty in understanding this, even now, under a system of landlordism that has reduced man to wage serfdom by depriving him of an alternative to entering the labor market. Locke was on safe ground in laying that basis for a just form of government. The following passage clinches firmly the idea he held of the purpose for which land was provided:

... God, when He gave the world in common to all mankind, commanded man also to labour, and the penury of his condition required it of him. God and his reason commanded him to subdue the earth—*i.e.*, improve it for the benefit of life and therein lay out something upon it that was his own, his labour. He that, in obedience to this command of God, subdued, tilled, and sowed any part of it, thereby annexed to it something that was his property, which another had no title to, nor could without injury take from him.

All this explanation, however, is far too simple for some of our modern economists to grasp. But Locke is not to be blamed for not seeing what enclosure by landowners would do to subject the dispossessed people to enter the labor market or starve. The objections that have been made to the way Locke has employed the term "appropriate" in connection with land are somewhat paltry, because in no part of the treatises does he countenance appropriation for ownership of a single yard of territory. The term "appropriate" is always concerned with the parcel required by man to satisfy his needs.

It is true that Locke did not clearly specify the conditions under the private ownership of land. Nevertheless, the principle that he laid down that land could be appropriated for use was not vitiated by the fact that many men had enclosed the land of England in great estates and forced others to cultivate it, or otherwise improve it, for the chief benefit of the owner. All this was quite contrary to the principles of appropriation for personal use upon which Locke based his system.

Why should Locke be criticized for realizing that man-made law is not according to the will of God? When he points out the exceptions to his fundamental principle of the use of land, he realizes that he has entered into another sphere of controversy, namely: the political power to deprive men of the right to use that which is necessary for their life. Still, in this respect he holds firmly to the basic principle he has laid down in regard to appropriating a piece of land for use. And he says:

> . . . For as a man had a right to all he could employ his labour upon, so he had no temptation to labour for more than he could make use of. This left no room for controversy about the title, nor for encroachment on the right of others. What portion a man carved to himself was easily seen; and it was useless, as well as dishonest, to carve himself too much, or take more than he needed.

Perhaps it is well for us that there is a revival of interest in the work of Locke because we have reached the stage when we should take soundings of our condition and attempt to chart a course we may be forced to follow before this generation is much older. Most of the civilizations of the past witnessed their great States decay and their vaunted empires fall to ruin. Wars brought chaos, and the historians of later times, reviewing the remains of their territories, saw that its ravages had reduced the survivors to the status of the fellaheen. As Spengler points out, man returned to his first calling and became a peasant.

In these unhappy days when the world strife cannot be ignored by the humblest creature in any country, the thoughtful people of the west might review the principles laid down by Locke and give them careful study. The menace of Communism brings the threat of another great war. The thought of it is enough to chill the bravest heart. The devastation that might be wrought by atomic bombs may bring our vaunted political enterprises, together with the magnificent monuments of our industry, to ruin in a few hours. It took long years to reduce the pagan empires to nothing. Some of them had a slow decline; but in these days of warfare, when science has supplied the arms of destruction, our cities may be laid waste before the people could migrate to places of probable security in the country. In such a case, those who could escape would not be able to take their possessions with them.

What, then—supposing a peace had come—would they do? Why, what else can be thought of than that of the husbandry of the peasant, just as it was in the pagan past? And, yet, there are powers still vested in the people that might be used to their advantage, if they knew what they were. As Lord Russell says, it is stupidity and ignorance that have brought us to this pass.

Strange as it may seem to such taxpayers as we are, we have the power to demand the redress of grievance before we grant supply for the purposes of government, whether in peace or in war. But to realize this, it is necessary for us to understand our rights and to learn that authority is in our hands, no matter what the form of government may be, and that the will of the people shall be expressed.

Salus populi suprema est lex, the welfare of the people is the supreme law. But as this is merely a figure of speech in the theory of constitutional government, there is no record of a modern civilization attempting to make it the practice of legislators. Indeed, it may be said that our democracies today, protecting landlordism, huckstering in nepotism, privilege, and preferment, seem to realize that the supreme law is to look after the welfare of some persons of political influence. Yet, even here today, in Great Britain, and in France, the legislative powers recognize that there must be a semblance of government by consent. However, it does not extend beyond the electoral system of adult suffrage. The people may select their representatives, and by a majority in the separate districts elect them for the legislature; but there their interest ends. A change of party in office makes little difference, so far as the purpose of government being the security of property and the welfare of the citizens is concerned.

The economic pressure seems to be too great upon the producers (whether they be in the category of labor or of capital) for them to learn once more that the supreme political power is still in their hands. The right to withhold supply until grievance is removed has not yet been filched from the mass of the people.

In the old days men had a far, far higher sense of their rights than they have now. There is a long history behind every revolt of the people against oppression, and Locke's treatment of this phase of government is well worth our study and reflection. Even in a democracy it is possible for the head of the government and his supporters to arrogate to themselves dictatorial powers. We have already seen that democratic rulers themselves, or through their ministers, can assume an arrogance that we despise in totalitarian dictators. Therefore, taxation without consent is a grievance that should be considered before supply is voted.

The history concerning the beginnings of this republic is an example of what can be done when the people decline to be taxed unjustly. The revolt against Charles Stuart, when John Hampden refused to pay the ship money tax, is another example. There were many before that period. Wolsey was ordered from the House of Commons by Sir Thomas More, the speaker, when he entered to demand a 20 per cent property tax.

In the archives of Lincoln Cathedral is recorded the story of its great abbot, Hugh, journeying as far as Caen, in France, to protest against the order of Richard I to tax the diocese. Hugh entered the cathedral where Richard was assembled with his knights, awaiting the ceremony of the Mass, and plucking the King's tunic, he said, "Revoke the order which you gave to seize and confiscate my possessions, and know the diocese of Lincoln is bound to furnish military service for the king, but only within the boundaries of England."

There were many brave prelates in that day. Behind all this, in the long history, we find the right to revolt incorporated in the Great Charter of John. The sixty-first article says:

> . . . It shall be lawful for every one in our realm to rise against us and to use all the ways and means they can to hinder us; to which we will that each and every one shall henceforth be bound by our command . . . so that they shall in no way give attention to us, but that they shall do everything which aims at our injury and shall in no way be bound to us, until that in which we have transgressed and offenced shall have been by a fitting satisfaction brought again into due state, according to the form of the ordinance of the aforesaid.

There it is, and if there be such a thing as legislative authority granted by the people to a ruler, the authority to revolt against grievance is basic in the constitution of English-speaking people. The last pages of the second treatise *Of Civil Government* might be studied more closely in such times as these.

Now the civilization of megalomaniacs has carried us far on the road to destruction, and in reflecting upon Locke's theory of government, the thought cannot be suppressed that he realized that the basis of a culture was the primary industry of producing necessaries for the well-being of the creature. There are passages which indicate the idea that a pastoral community was not only the wise one for men to pursue, but that it was nearer to the wisdom of God in providing for the happiness of His children.

Still, no matter how this point may be regarded, we must realize that we cannot have it both ways. The higher a civilization is developed, the further man is divorced from the source of his well-being. And shrewd thinkers today ponder the awful problem of the landless man. Ortega and others have warned us of the perils of our condition, but only a few—very few—of our philosophers seem to have taken on the duties of the priesthood of other days.

Yet, light is breaking in upon clouded minds, and some are beginning to understand that the human basis of a political democracy is a landless proletariat. If we wish to avoid the abyss that is yawning, the horrors of war with the devastating accoutrements of science, we should think, and think deeply; and perhaps there is no one better qualified to give us enlightenment of our true position than John Locke.

IV

Kant's Law of Freedom

THERE IS NOTHING QUITE LIKE A WAR WITH A FOREIGN State for opening up an opportunity to belligerent patriots to make use of the concept "freedom." Indeed, it is like an old-fashioned Fourth of July, when orators in every town and village delivered speeches about the founding of this Republic. Then, this word "freedom" was played upon with the *vox humana* stop pulled out, and the throb of the eloquence of the local Demosthenes stirred the congregations to their very depths.

Surely the notion of freedom must have meant more to the people of two generations ago than it does to the masses of our day. Yet, it may be inferred that it was not necessary sixty years ago to ask an orator who used the term what he meant by it. If he were questioned, I can imagine that he would readily reply that it was what was gained by the American people when they threw off the Hanoverian yoke. And a very sensible reply that would be.

During the past two World Wars I have often wondered what would happen if any man were so bold as to ask our politicians, our editors, and our pulpiteers what the term really meant to them. For it must be acknowledged even by modern philosophers and historians that war is a denial of freedom. Although we may enter a conflict against a foreign power because it denies the principles of democracy and we fight in the name of freedom, the righteous nation begins to lose whatever freedom it has, just as soon as the war starts. It is not

51

necessary to quote the thinkers who have laid down maxims and axioms on this point. I think it will be conceded that those philosophers who have told us that freedom is lost when war begins have been right; at least, history confirms the conclusion they have reached.

Now this loss to the righteous nation is in so many cases a political and social one that we overlook the deeper loss of spiritual and economic advantages enjoyed in days of peace. The restrictions that curtail our political and social freedom do not end there, for all activities of life are affected and suffer grievously. After World War I when the shocking consequences were patent to everyone who had the capacity to observe what had taken place, the moralists gave us volume after volume, lamenting the grave state of affairs wrought by the restraints that had been placed upon the people. Now those who have the courage to describe the consequences of World War II depict a condition such as was never conceived by the medieval artists who gave us representations of hell itself.

I have recently read several books on various aspects of the war and how certain States suffered the loss of freedom. Three works on Poland and one dealing with the expeditions in Finland and the Baltic States—all reveal that freedom was the issue. Over and over again we meet the phrase: "We fought for freedom."

Strangely enough, the authors of those books I have looked through do not saddle the whole responsibility for the loss of freedom in many European States upon the wicked enemies that we fought. They indicate that our own government was not blameless in many cases. Indeed, it is suggested that the righteous Allies practiced not only downright mendacity but a reckless breaking of solemn pledges.

Perhaps it might be just as well at this time for us to give thought to the matter of what freedom is, and how it can be defined so that the ordinary taxpayer will be able to understand it; for to him it is a most expensive political luxury, and often brings him face to face with spiritual and material ruin.

Side by side with the books published by politicians and diplomatists of the various States affected by the war, there have come from the presses many notable volumes from the pens of philosophers, which deal with this bothersome word "freedom." One work that will help to purge the mind of its political and social dross and make for a healthier spiritual outlook is the Gifford Lectures of Dr. W. Macneile Dixon, entitled *The Human Situation*. It is an exhilarating analysis of conditions as they exist, although the lectures were delivered in the University of Glasgow in 1938. Not for a long time has anything so virile come to my notice.

There is also *The Myth of the State*, by Dr. Ernst Cassirer, which is a particularly illuminating record of the vicissitudes suffered by political freedom since classical times. These authors do not pretend to have discovered what the word really means, but a far better conception of it may be gathered from a study of their two books than is to be found in volumes written by politicians and diplomatists. If we desire to delve more deeply into the meaning of this term, we must perforce seek what knowledge we can gather of it in other channels of thought.

The first work I should like to bring to the notice of the reader is *Ideas Have Consequences*, by Richard M. Weaver. It is, in the main, a diagnosis of the religious and cultural decline of western civilization. The author draws a distressing picture of the welter of strifes under which we exist, brought about not by "biological or other necessity but of unintelligent choice." He assumes that we live in an intelligible world and that man is free, but he does not tell us directly of what this freedom consists. We are left to infer from his survey that the actions of men who have contributed to this decline have been free only in a very limited way. He realizes, however, that: "There is ground for declaring that modern man has become a moral idiot."

Mr. Weaver is an unusual critic, for he reveals in his book that he is spiritually and intellectually equipped to conduct the clinical examination of the west, now sick unto death. Yet, I doubt whether the cure he prescribes will set the patient on its legs again and restore to it that vigor expressed in the long past, when religious social, and cultural miracles were wrought. He says in conclusion:

> It may be that we are awaiting a great change, that the sins of the fathers are going to be visited upon the generations until the reality of evil is again brought home and there comes some passionate reaction, like that which flowered in the chivalry and spirituality of the Middle Ages. If such is the most we can hope for, something toward that revival may be prepared by acts of thought and volition in this waning day of the West.

To accomplish this essential change, he depends very much on what he calls "personality," to which term he gives a meaning that differs somewhat from the one accepted by philosophers several generations ago. One of the prevalent sins of our moral philosophers is that they take many leading words and give them alien meanings. This tendency to twist or reshape the meaning of leading terms is causing much confusion of thought. In some cases, I find it is done palpably to adjust the sense of a word to the fortuitous circumstances which exist, with the result that a new connotation is given to it. Philosophical and economic terms suffer severely from this abuse.

Such a term is "personality." Mr. Weaver says that in its true definition it is theomorphic. This is stretching a meaning out of all shape. Why it should be so defined we are not told, but the term is presented to us in contradistinction to that other abused one—"individuality"—which for some unexplained reason he regards with contempt. He writes:

. . . Individualism, with its connotation of irresponsibility, is a direct invitation to selfishness, and all that this treatise has censured can be traced in some way to individualist mentality.

This is quite a new way of defining individualism, and our author would be hard put to it to explain clearly to any philosopher of the nineteenth century why the term should be used so opprobriously. Two generations ago, an individual (even in a social sense) was regarded as a person of esteem and distinction, and one guilty of the offense suggested by Mr. Weaver was either a bounder or a criminal.

But this notion does not originate with our author. It came into fashion with the advent of the Fabians, who realized that the individual—or individualism— was antagonistic to socialistic doctrine. It may be news to Mr. Weaver that a generation ago there were many debates on "Individualism versus Socialism." I think it may be held that the individualists in America at the time of the founding of this Republic were those who had a far better knowledge of right and political freedom than the bureaucrats of the government in London. If the true definition of the term personality is "theomorphic," there is no reason why individuality should not be so. For there can be no personality without the individual.

Unfortunately for us, millions are born into this world who seldom bear the stamp of an individual, for they never have the opportunity to develop themselves. The one great factor which is an obstacle to this is the economic condition in which these people are placed. And, as it is in so many books that have been written in recent years, there is no practical suggestion in *Ideas Have Consequences* as to how they are to work out their own salvation. Indeed, it may be said today that the millions of small wage earners have been taught by their political mentors to look to the State to relieve them of all responsibility. They are now regarded as mere automata, essential in the industrial process which denudes them of individuality and, therefore, leaves them no chance whatever of cultivating a personality. Mr. Weaver continues:

> . . . But personality is that little private area of selfhood in which the person is at once conscious of his relationship to the transcendental and the living community. He is a particular vessel, but he carries some part of the universal mind. . . . There is piety in the belief that personality, like the earth we tread on, is something given us.

I am inclined to agree with this statement, but I cannot dissociate his idea from that of individuality. Before the term "personality" became popular with the moral philosophers of our day, individuals of worth possessed the attributes that are now given to this nebulous something called personality. If it is to be described as "piety" (in the old sense it bore), then there is no difficulty in comprehending the meaning of the term. Perhaps what millions in the world lack is the pious mind, one that appreciates the bounty of the Creator and realizes that the good life may be sought in observing the divine law, as it was interpreted by the inspired teachers of all religions.

Notwithstanding the exceptions that I take to Mr. Weaver's book, it is one that should be carefully studied by those who understand the mighty problems that confront us and desire to find a way out of the chaos created by the unthinking.

The next work I would present for consideration is Bronislaw Malinowski's *Freedom and Civilization*. The title is something of an anachronism, for to my mind the latter destroys the former. The very fact that bureaucracies increase as civilizations grow when, under a system of taxation of wealth, producers are exploited for the upkeep of the State, indicates there can be little freedom. Perhaps what is left of it is limited to the electoral badge of voting for one bureaucrat or the other. Malinowski agrees that no clear definition has been formulated. He quotes Professor Walton Hamilton of the Yale Law School, who says: "For all our knowledge and understanding, we can no more define freedom than we can realize it."

Presumably Mr. Weaver would be surprised to learn from Malinowski:

> Freedom in individual existence is this selection of specific differential bondage. Freedom however is very real; it is the range in molding the individual's existence, in choice of mate, career, hobby, creed and art; it is the organization of opportunities, the supply of wherewithal, the range of initiative in creative change. This is the treasure-house of freedom in democratic cultures.

Let us concede that the choice of mate may be accepted as an example of freedom, but I doubt very much indeed whether the millions would agree with our noted anthropologist that there is much choice in the matter of a career, a creed, or art. Moreover, I question the range of initiative for the masses, and as for "the organization of opportunities," in a democracy such as this, they are reserved in great part for the politicians and their friends. At least, it has been so for the past fifteen years.

Freedom and Civilization is what the critics call a provocative work. It really does make one think, because so much of it is in the nature of a challenge to many of the latter-day sociologists. Malinowski considers that: "Freedom is closely related to the proto-democratic, and in historical times, to the democratic constitution of culture." He goes further still and asserts:

> . . . Freedom in fact is essential to the survival of culture at its earliest stages. Culture, let us repeat, is a gift of this early freedom. All means, technical and intellectual, and social achievements are at the very primitive levels embodied in the members of the group. Culture lives in their memories, in their acts, in their forms of organization.

There can be little doubt about this although so many men of our period have been under the impression that the cultural monuments we revere in States east and west were raised by serfs. In this respect it surely must be held that it is merely a relative term. For what man today, who must compete for a job in the labor market, join a union, and be under the dictatorship of a labor czar, would not change places as a politically free man with the serf of the Middle Ages who had twelve acres, a hut, privileges in the lord's forests and could earn sufficient in thirteen weeks to keep himself and family for a year?

During the past twenty years scores of books have been written by authors of repute on this question of freedom. Philosophers, economists, physicists, historians, and sociologists are only a few of the learned people who have tried their hands and minds at elucidating for us an understandable definition. Nothing seems to fit the rapidly changing conditions of the period. One of the reasons for this is expressed by Malinowski:

> . . . This unpreparedness is natural since democracy is the denial of both war and preparedness. Total war is the most fundamental contradiction of everything which a democracy believes to be true, real and valuable.

And, yet, our rulers war to suppress totalitarianism and, in so doing, are obliged to place its chains upon us who enjoy a modicum of freedom. A war in our day seems to be the best way to cultivate the obnoxious thing. There is something wrong with the reasoning of those authors who think that freedom is to be preserved by going to war to destroy totalitarianism in an enemy State. Curiously enough, Malinowski lays it down clearly that freedom may be defined as "the smooth and effective, as well as successful, run of an activity undertaken by a group of men who with a clear aim in view combine for the task, fit themselves out for action and achieve the desired end."

But both the Russians and the Germans, before the last war began, could have subscribed to this without compunction. The deeper we go into this matter of trying to discover what freedom is, the less chance there seems to be of finding it.

It will be a shock to many of the adherents of libertarian ideas to learn from Malinowski that discipline and drill are essential in a free system. He says that "no human culture can exist without the factor of discipline, with *force as its ultimate sanction.*" (italics mine)

However, it is not to be inferred that Malinowski has reference to the discipline exercised by Hitler or a Stalin. A democratic discipline is preferable, but all we have to do to get the measure of such a course in a democracy is to walk down a busy street and notice the behavior of the people on foot and those who are in vehicles. Democrats using the revolving doors of a department store or an office building may give one an idea of the difficulties to be confronted in an attempt to impose discipline upon the herd. Washington itself, in and out of Congress, is a notorious example of lack of discipline.

I recommend *Freedom and Civilization* because it comes from the mind of a scientist, and in its analysis of this term differs widely from any other work I have seen.

The exegetists of our day have departed far from the idea of freedom that was held by Moses and Joshua— two of our oldest experimentalists who are worthy of all respect. They had known what slavery was and were eager to enter a promised land where there would be no more of it. The imperatives of the Decalogue were explained to the children by Moses who changed hordes of slaves into a people prepared to obey the commandments of God. At Sinai "all the people answered together and said: All that the Lord has spoken we will do."

After a while they were tired of obedience, and some generations later they were obliged to obey the imperatives of the Code of Hammurabi.

But since the day of the disobedient children, we have had many philosophers who have left us records of what they thought about freedom. Since Plato there have been innumerable men in all European States who have gathered the best that has been thought and said upon this term, and none greater than Kant himself. Perhaps it is time that our instructors in the universities should revive the old slogan, "Back to Kant!" I seem to remember such philosophers as Stirling, Caird, Calderwood, and several others using this slogan, or words that conveyed the same notion, and when I think of them and their zeal for downright knowledge of the subject, I am bewildered at the utter confusion of the men of our day who use this term freedom so frivolously.

Perhaps a revival of Kantian studies is due, for several excellent works about him from philosophers of great attainment have been produced in recent years. The last one to come to my notice is from the mind of Dr. H. J. Paton, a Fellow of the British Academy and White's Professor of Moral Philosophy in the University of Oxford. It is called *The Categorical Imperative, A Study in Kant's Moral Philosophy.* If this work did no more than purge away the stupid confusions that have choked a clear understanding of Kant's philosophy, it would serve an excellent purpose. For the notions that some professors have held of Kant are so far from a true appreciation that it is small wonder many have gone astray. Dr. Paton says:

> . . . It is indeed a strange thing that so many of those who either explicitly or implicitly regard Kant as a great, or at least an influential, thinker, ascribe to him views which can hardly be considered as anything but silly. Thus he is commonly supposed to maintain that no action can be moral if we have any natural inclination towards it or if we obtain the slightest pleasure from its performance; and again that a

good man must take no account whatever of the consequences of his actions but must deduce all the manifold duties of life from the bare conception of moral law as such—without any regard for the characteristics of human nature or the circumstances of human life. These doctrines and others equally paradoxical, if they were held by Kant, would not indicate that he had any very profound insight into the nature of morality.

A list of names of men who have blundered would include not a few modern philosophers and sociologists.

Paton takes the *Groundwork of the Metaphysic of Morals*, and he shows how the moral philosophy fits in with other parts of the critical doctrine. Beginning with Kant's declaration: "It is impossible to conceive anything in the world, or even out of it, which can be taken as good without limitation, save only a *good will*," our author proceeds to apply the critical method to the statement, and the task he sets for himself in attempting to accomplish this feat is an achievement of high worth. In the exercise of this philosophical excursion many of the misconceptions of Kant's purpose and doctrine are cleared up. Kant held that *"principles without content are empty, impulses without concepts are blind."* (italics mine)

In the sixth chapter of *The Categorical Imperative*, entitled "The Law," Dr. Paton says:

> *Universality* is the essential characteristic of law as such. A law, in the strict sense of "law," must hold for all cases and admit of no exceptions. A law of nature, for example, must hold of all events in time without exception. If the principle that every event must have a cause is a law of nature, then there can be no exceptions to it; and if we were convinced that any exceptions were possible, we should at once deny this principle to be a law of nature. So it is also with what Kant calls "the law of freedom"—that is, the law in accordance with which a rational agent would act if reason had full control over his inclinations. This law of freedom, or moral law, cannot have exceptions without ceasing to be law. There cannot be one moral law for me and another for you. The law must be the same for all.

Such an idea could never be put into practice by political governments. Indeed, this freedom is not for the group; it is for the individual. Once we bring reason, in the Kantian sense, to bear upon this concept, we must conclude that the freedom we talk about so lightly concerns merely our goings and comings in the routine of daily existence. It never seems to get beyond political bounds. Our author continues:

> The Idea of freedom is a concept which pure reason cannot but entertain; yet if we suppose, as many do, that this Idea can give us knowledge of any reality, we fall into illusion. The supposedly real use of pure reason in this way is very natural, and even irresistible, but it does not thereby cease to be illusory. . . .

I know of no work upon Kant that presents the imperatives so clearly as Dr. Paton's. There has been so much misunderstanding of what these are and the way they should be interpreted that I strongly urge students of philosophy to follow Paton's examination of them. At the risk of being wearisome in a short review, I shall present them in the form set down in *The Categorical Imperative:*

Formula I or the Formula of Universal Law:

Act only on that maxim through which you can at the same time will that it should become a universal law.

Formula Ia or the Formula of the Law of Nature:

Act as if the maxim of your action were to become through your will a UNIVERSAL LAW OF NATURE.

Formula II or the Formula of the End in Itself:

So act as to use humanity, both in your own person and in the person of every other, always at the same time as an end, never simply as a means.

Formula III or the Formula of Autonomy:

So act that your will can regard itself at the same time as making universal law through its maxim.

Formula IIIa or the Formula of the Kingdom of Ends:
So act as if you were always through your maxims a law-making member in a universal kingdom of ends.

It will be seen that the Universal Law of Freedom, as pronounced in the Imperative, will never get beyond the philosophical mind. The first step toward a realization of this utopia is the cultivation of a good will, and that is far to seek today. Dr. Paton writes:

. . . This good or rational will Kant takes to be present in every rational agent, and so in every man, however much it may be overlaid by irrationality. Hence man, and indeed every rational agent as such, must be said to exist as an end in itself, one which should never be used simply as a means to the realisation of some end whose value is merely relative.

It will be a surprise to many of those who hold false notions of Kant's so-called rationalism to learn that

. . . His Formula of Universal Law, insisting as it does on the spirit as opposed to the letter of the moral law, is his version of the Christian doctrine that we are saved by faith and not by works. His formula of the End in Itself is his way of expressing the Christian view that every individual human being has a unique and infinite value and should be treated as such. His Formula of the Kingdom of Ends as a Kingdom of Nature is quite explicitly his rational form of recognising a church invisible and visible, the Kingdom of God which has to be made manifest on earth.

Dr. Paton holds that "Kant is very much nearer to that original doctrine than is commonly supposed." But in dealing with the problem of the utility of the imperatives, he says:

It is sheer error to suggest that Kant is trying to explain how pure reason can be practical or how freedom can be possible. These questions Kant has not only refrained from answering: he roundly asserts that they are beyond the power of human reason to answer.

Kant was a pioneer, the first who contrived to say something new about morality, and so far no one has

succeeded in presenting a better performance. To inter-
link morality and freedom with good will was a remarkable achievement.

This brief review of *The Categorical Imperative* is
intended to bring Dr. Paton's monograph to the notice
of those who have found it difficult to formulate an
idea of freedom, which will be of service in the chaotic
condition brought about by the war. However, I do
not expect that many students will find it easy to read
his book.

I would therefore recommend what I consider to be a
work that might be called "First Steps to the Understanding of Kant's Metaphysic of Morals." It contains
the "Lectures on Ethics" given by Kant in 1780-81 and
goes by that title. To celebrate the bicentenary of the
philosopher's birth, the Kant-Gesellschaft took three
students' notebooks and drew from them a volume
which was published in Germany in 1924. The English
translation by Louis Infield was brought out by the
Century Company in 1930.

The lectures deal with a wide range of subjects, and
it is surprising how easily they are read and understood.
They afford the necessary equipment for young scholars
who will venture to read Dr. Paton's work. No doubt it
will be gathered from both the volumes that it is high
time our practical men who have made such a mess of
things should turn to the philosopher and learn from
him how to do something to help our youth to cultivate
the good will Kant calls for as the essential of understanding the Imperatives of the Universal Law of
Freedom.

V

Goethe—"Voilà un homme!"

GREAT BRITAIN AND THE UNITED STATES RECENTLY celebrated the two hundredth anniversary of the birth of the author of *Faust*. This event was one of the few signs of the return of wisdom in the cultural sphere. No matter what has happened in the past thirty-five years to blot from our memory the real debt we owe to Goethe, it is to be hoped the celebrations will go far toward re-establishing the relationships that united European people in all that was best in philosophy, literature, and art. So far as we are concerned, it is our humble duty to associate with the name of the great German poet that of Bayard Taylor, who gave to the English-speaking world the worthy translation of *Faust*, with voluminous notes of inestimable value.

How strange it is to look back some two generations and read once more the chorus of praise rendered by English and American authors to an artist who lived and worked in the days of their fathers. To be extolled, as he was, by so many of the highly cultured critics of that extraordinary period—rich in poets—is a unique experience.

When one reads the tribute penned to him in that fascinating work, *The Maclise Portrait Gallery*, it does not seem possible that the world of men could go mad and forget so soon the illustrious past. To be reminded, as we are in this essay, of the many famous authors in America and in England who paid homage to Goethe is something of a shock to those of us who have lived through the wars of the twentieth century.

Dr. John Robertson, who wrote the article upon him in *The Encyclopædia Britannica*, says:

> . . . Of all modern men, Goethe is the most universal type of genius. It is the full, rich humanity of his life and personality—not the art behind which the artist disappears, of the definite pronouncements of the thinker or the teacher—that constitutes his claim to a place in the front rank of men of letters. His life was his greatest work.

In the field of state politics, studied so little by many of his biographers, he stands out as a statesman of unusual character. In the theater, he was a master of the dramatist's craft, a thorough journeyman of the technique of the stage, and an eminent *régisseur*. Few have grasped the fact that he was a political economist of exceptional merit; in the sphere of science, he was a predecessor of Darwin, and his investigations into botany and anatomy yielded some contributions that are now considered to be surprisingly original. His mind was universal in scope. Fearlessly he entered realms of thought that were forbidden to many of his famous contemporaries. To be influenced by Kant and Schiller meant much to Goethe; but to be accepted in so many fields of learning was rare to one whose reputation was made as a poet.

Despite the adverse criticism of the second part of *Faust*, which came from such Goethe scholars as Hayward, Lewes, and many lesser lights, it must be remembered that the "Helena" fantasy was written long before he set to work upon the final scenes of the tragedy. Indeed, in 1828, Carlyle wrote a review of it that runs to more than fifty pages in the *Critical and Miscellaneous Essays*. It was the incorporation of this scene in *Faust* that mystified so many of the German and English critics. But, somehow, Carlyle saw in it a work of eerie imagination and wrote:

. . . It is wonderful with what fidelity the Classical style is maintained throughout the earlier part of the Poem; how skilfully it is at once united to the Romantic style of the latter part and made to reappear, at intervals, to the end.

However, the acrimonious debate that arose when the second part was published in its entirety is now forgotten, and Bayard Taylor himself nearly eighty years ago could say:

The early disparagement which the Second Part of *Faust* received is only in our day beginning to give way to an intelligent recognition of its grand design, its wealth of illustration, and the almost inexhaustible variety and beauty of its rhythmical forms.

It may not be amiss to point out that the end of the second part of *Faust* is the culmination of the thoughts expressed in the early scenes of the first part. In the Prologue in Heaven, the scheme is subtly announced by the archangels Raphael, Gabriel, and Michael:

The ocean-tides in foam are breaking,
Against the rocks' deep bases hurled,
And both, the spheric race partaking,
Eternal, swift, are onward whirled!
And rival storms abroad are surging
From sea to land, from land to sea,
A chain of deepest action forging
Round all, in wrathful energy.
There flames a desolation, blazing
Before the Thunder's crashing way:
Yet, Lord, Thy messengers are praising
The gentle movement of Thy Day.
Though still by them uncomprehended,
From these the angels draw their power,
And all Thy works, sublime and splendid,
Are bright as in Creation's hour.

It is in the Prologue, also, that we learn something of the condition of the world of man, and the description given to the Lord by Mephistopheles might be served as an indictment now of the wreck man has made of his heritage.

He portrays the depravity of the fallen creature thus:

The little god o' the world sticks to the same old way,
And is as whimsical as on Creation's day.
Life somewhat better might content him,
But for the gleam of heavenly light which Thou has lent him:
He calls it Reason—thence his power's increased,
To be far beastlier than any beast.
Saving Thy Gracious Presence, he to me
A long-legged grasshopper appears to be,
That springing flies, and flying springs,
And in the grass the same old ditty sings.
Would he still lay among the grass he grows in!
Each bit of dung he seeks, to stick his nose in.

The Lord asks:

Hast thou, then, nothing more to mention?
Com'st ever, thus, with ill intention?
Find'st nothing right on earth, eternally?

And Mephistopheles replies:

No, Lord! I find things, there, still bad as they can be.
Man's misery even to pity moves my nature;
I've scarce the heart to plague the wretched creature.

Then comes the test of the power of the devil to triumph everlastingly over the soul of man. The Lord selects Faust for the purpose, and the wager is made as to who will win him in the end. Mephistopheles describes his victim as one frenzied, reaching to the fairest stars, to the highest raptures, and unable to subdue the tumult of his breast. However, the Lord says:

Though still confused his service unto Me,
I soon shall lead him to a clearer morning.
Sees not the gardener, even while buds his tree,
Both flower and fruit the future years adorning?

In the monologue which opens the drama, Faust submits himself to searching self-examination and decides that all his learning amounts to a "rummage in empty words." Suddenly his dejection is pierced by a flashing inspiration, and he cries, "Fly! Up, and seek the broad, free land!"

It is important to mark this exclamation because it is a keynote which must be kept firmly in mind all through the two parts of the drama, and it leads to the great culmination that is reached in the final scene of the second part. It is remarkable that so many of the poet's greatest admirers have missed this dominant motif and have said so little about the meaning of the triumph of Faust proclaimed in the death speech which closes the tragedy. Even so thorough a disciple of the poet as Bayard Taylor fails to give the slightest inkling of an understanding of the victory Faust attains at the end.

The first part of the drama is fairly well known. But how seldom one finds a student who has given close study to the second part. Perhaps it is the romance of Margaret in the earlier section that grips the mind, and when she passes from the scene it is not easy to revive an interest in the sublime finale of the tragedy. And, yet, the poem is incomplete at that stage. For in the second part, the turmoil of the world is laid bare, and the spiritual struggle of Faust is the test he must survive if Mephistopheles is to lose his wager. Those whose souls have been bruised by the horror of events in recent years cannot afford to neglect reading Part II, particularly Acts IV and V. There is scarcely a problem of universal importance that is not dealt with in these scenes.

Faust and Mephistopheles are present at the court where the Emperor is surrounded by his chiefs-of-state. He has been told that the earth is his; indeed, he compares his reign to a tale from *A Thousand and One Nights*. The High Steward says: "Things can't in Heaven more cheerful be." And as for the armed forces, the General-in-Chief announces:

> Arrears of pay are settled duly,
> The army is enlisted newly;
> The trooper's blood is all alive,
> The landlords and the wenches thrive.

But how has all this good fortune come about? It is so miraculous that the Emperor himself feels a little disturbed at such a change. The Chancellor then explains the magical fiscal trick of issuing paper as a temporary device to save the State from bankruptcy:

> In my old days I'm blest, and most content.
> So hear and see the fortune-freighted leaf
> Which has transformed to happiness our grief.
> "To all to whom this cometh, be it known:
> A thousand crowns in worth this note doth own.
> It to secure, as certain pledge, shall stand
> All buried treasure in the Emperor's land:
> And 't is decreed, perfecting thus the scheme,
> The treasure, soon as raised, shall this redeem."

Just a few strokes of the pen, a wide distribution of the paper in payment of wage, and the trick is done! Yet, the poor old Emperor is so puzzled about it all that he asks:

> And with my people does it pass for gold?
> For pay in court and camp, the notes they hold?
> Then I must yield, although the thing's amazing.

This scene describes our own present situation. Indeed, the satirical passages of statecraft and political thievery are worth serious study, for there was not a fiscal trick played then that is not being played by all States now.

It is in the fourth act that we find the theme of the archangels in the Prologue of the first part taking hold of the mind of Faust:

> The Sea sweeps on, in thousand quarters flowing,
> Itself unfruitful, barrenness bestowing;
> It breaks and swells, and rolls, and overwhelms
> The desert stretch of desolated realms.
> There endless waves hold sway, in strength erected

And then withdrawn,—and nothing is effected.
If aught could drive me to despair, 't were, truly
The aimless force of elements unruly.
Then dared my mind its dreams to over-soar:
Here would I fight,—subdue this fierce uproar!
And possible 't is!—Howe'er the tides may fill,
They gently fawn around the steadfast hill;
A moderate height resists and drives asunder,
A moderate depth allures and leads them on.
So, swiftly, plans within my mind were drawn:
Let that high joy be mine forevermore,
To shut the lordly Ocean from the shore,
The watery waste to limit and to bar,
And push it back upon itself afar!
From step to step I settled how to fight it:
Such is my wish: dare thou to expedite it!

Soon are heard the drums of war, and in what follows, the art of statecraft is laid bare with merciless clarity; hate and war, as we have known them in our day, appear in fierce habiliments, differing little from those specters that have haunted us. This extraordinary scene ends with a comment by Mephistopheles, which we should ponder deeply:

Firm in transmitted hate they anchor,
And show implacably their rancor:
Now far and wide the noise hath rolled.
At last, the Devils find a hearty
Advantage in the hate of Party,
Till dread and ruin end the tale:
Repulsive sounds of rage and panic,
With others, piercing and Satanic,
Resound along the frightened vale!

After the battle is fought, the Emperor and Archbishop discuss the matter of the division of the spoil. It differs little from what took place after World War I. Those who had helped to win the victory for the Emperor are to be rewarded according to service rendered:

You I award, ye Faithful, many a lovely land,
Together with the right, as you may have occasion,

> To spread them by exchange, or purchase, or invasion:
> Then be it clearly fixed, that you unhindered use
> Whate'er prerogatives have been the landlord's dues.
> When ye, as Judges, have the final sentence spoken,
> By no appeal from your high Court shall it be broken:
> Then levies, tax and rent, pass-money, tolls and fees
> Are yours,—of mines and salt and coin the royalties.

Acts IV and V must be read, for it is almost impossible in an essay to describe even a small part of the subjects dealt with or to show how the mighty aim of Faust survives all the bitterness of his thwarted life. That the idea of the vast plan lives through it all and comes to development is something of a miracle, and here the master poet's art of sustaining the interest in scenes of great complexity reaches the very apex of craftsmanship.

The beginning of the last act introduces Faust-Goethe as the Wanderer meeting Baucis and Philemon. In these two short scenes we have a glimpse of a past that the poet never forgot. The sylvan peace and contentment and simple trust of gentle souls in the goodness of God are so genuine in feeling that even the skeptic must be touched by their beauty. Again the prophetic strain of the mighty plan is struck, and Philemon describes the future state envisioned by Faust:

> Where the savage waves maltreated
> You, on shores of breaking foam,
> See, a garden lies completed,
> Like an Eden-dream of home!
> Old was I no longer eager,
> Helpful, as the younger are:
> And when I had lost my vigor,
> Also was the wave afar.
> Wise lords set their serfs in motion,
> Dikes upraised and ditches led,
> Minishing the rights of Ocean,
> Lords to be in Ocean's stead.
> See the green of many a meadow,
> Field and garden, wood and town!
> Come, our table waits in shadow!
> For the sun is going down.

Sails afar are gliding yonder;
Nightly to the port they fare:
To their nest the sea-birds wander,
For a harbor waits them there.
Distant now, thou hardly seëst
Where the Sea's blue arc is spanned,—
Right and left, the broadest, freest
Stretch of thickly-peopled land.

This is placed like a bright beacon to lighten our way through the dark passages of spiritual stress and physical pain that we encounter in the supreme struggle, which ends in the death triumph.

The glories of kingdoms and of empires are the talismans of Mephistopheles. The personification of Evil describes the ancient imperial way of going about the business ruthlessly:

Free is the mind on Ocean free;
Who there can ponder sluggishly?
You only need a rapid grip:
You catch a fish, you seize a ship;
And when you once are lord of three,
The fourth is grappled easily;
The fifth is then in evil plight;
You have the Power, and thus the Right.
You count the *What*, and not the *How:*
If I have ever navigated,
War, Trade and Piracy, I vow,
Are three in one, and can't be separated!

But he surfeits Faust with the attractions of these baubles that bring to him only the spirits of Want, Guilt, Necessity, and Care:

What though One Day with rational brightness beams,
The Night entangles us in webs of dreams.
From our young field of life we come, elate:
There croaks a bird: what croaks he? Evil fate!

Blinded by Care, who breathes in his face, and conscious that night is deepening about him, he cries:

Up from your couches, vassals, man by man!
Make grandly visible my daring plan!
Seize now your tools, with spade and shovel press!
The work traced out must be a swift success.
Quick diligence, severest ordering
The most superb reward shall bring;
And, that the mighty work completed stands,
One mind suffices for a thousand hands.

Then, old and tottering, he rejoices to hear the clat-
tering spade. The turbulent waves will be thrust back,
and notwithstanding the skepticism of Mephistopheles
who scorns the idea of a moat to protect the land and
predicts that it will prove to be *a grave*, Faust rises to
his soul's height and proclaims:

Below the hills a marshy plain
Infects what I so long have been retrieving;
This stagnant pool likewise to drain
Were now my latest and my best achieving.
To many millions let me furnish soil,
Though not secure, yet free to active toil;
Green, fertile fields, where men and herds go forth
At once, with comfort, on the newest Earth,
And swiftly settled on the hill's firm base,
Created by the bold, industrious race.
A land like Paradise here, round about:
Up to the brink the tide may roar without,
And though it gnaw, to burst with force the limit,
By common impulse all unite to hem it.
Yet! to this thought I hold with firm persistence;
The last result of wisdom stamps it true:
He only earns his freedom and existence,
Who daily conquers them anew.
Thus here, by dangers girt, shall glide away
Of childhood, manhood, age, the vigorous day:
And such a throng I fain would see,—
Stand on free soil among a people free!
Then dared I hail the Moment fleeing:
"Ah, still delay—thou art so fair!"
The traces cannot, of mine earthly being,
In æons perish,—they are there!—
In proud fore-feeling of such lofty bliss,
I now enjoy the highest Moment,—this!

The end of this death triumph is like an echo of the declaration given by Faust in Act I of the first part, when the terms of the wager were settled:

> When thus I hail the Moment flying:
> "Ah, still delay—thou art so fair!"
> Then bind me in thy bonds undying,
> My final ruin then declare!
> Then let the death-bell chime the token,
> Then art thou from thy service free!
> The clock may stop, the hand be broken,
> Then Time be finished unto me!

And so at the end, when Faust dies, the memory of the thought that came to him when he made the wager startles us:

> *Mephistopheles.*
>
> No joy could sate him, and suffice no bliss!
> To catch but shifting shapes was his endeavor:
> The latest, poorest, emptiest Moment—this,—
> He wished to hold it fast forever.
> Me he resisted in such vigorous wise,
> But Time is lord, on earth the old man lies.
> The clock stands still—
>
> *Chorus.*
>
> Stands still; silent as midnight, now!
> The index falls.
>
> *Mephistopheles.*
>
> It falls; and it is finished, here!
>
> *Chorus.*
>
> 'T is past!
>
> *Mephistopheles.*
>
> —Past! a stupid word.
> If past, then why?
> Past and pure Naught, complete monotony!
> What good for us, this endlessly creating?—
> What is created then annihilating?
> "And now it's past!" Why read a page so twisted?
> 'T is just the same as if it ne'er existed,
> Yet goes in circles round as if it had, however:
> I'd rather choose, instead, the Void forever.

Bayard Taylor tells us in a note that it was a favorite maxim of Goethe that no man can really possess that which he has not personally acquired. This idea approximates the Justinian definition of property, and no doubt the poet saw clearly the difference between land—the created source of all wealth, man's subsistence—and the produce gained by his labor for his well-being.

In understanding this, we realize what the aged Faust intends to convey when he says:

> He only earns his freedom and existence,
> Who daily conquers them anew.

It is wonderful to see how Goethe is in agreement with the same ideas expressed by Byron and Shelley; and that his thought upon this fundamental question differs little from that of Leibnitz and, later, Kant. Eckermann tells us that in 1831 Goethe said:

> Let men continue to worship Him who gives the ox his pasture, and to man food and drink, according to his need. But I worship Him, who has filled the world with such a productive energy, that, if only the millionth part became embodied in living existence, the globe would so swarm with them that War, Pestilence, Flood and Fire would be powerless to diminish them. That is *my* God!

Here is one with the pagan toiler who raised an altar at which he might worship the Author of his being and give thanks for the source of his subsistence. This yearning for action and fruitfulness runs through the whole tragedy as a cosmic strain of melody courses through the heavens, giving joy to the stars. The Faustian spirit is expressed dynamically in the desire for more and still more knowledge, and acts like a tonic stimulating effort to mightier aims. This is the physical Faust—Man in actuality; but the spiritual Faust—poet and sufferer—is not defeated by the titanic physical forces of the world.

How beautifully Goethe blends the symbolism of the soul's high yearning to reach the Godhead with the storm and stress of worldly endeavor! The profound mind of the poet conceives the laws of nature as an attribute of divine justice, which should regulate the ordinances of life. The good tidings may be expressed in a line—subsistence for body and elevation for soul. Hence, a free soil for a people free, with war banished and pestilence subdued. A nobler theme can scarcely be imagined, and if we have stressed this motive of the sublime tragedy more than others have done, it is because we find in it so much that concerns the affairs of our world at this hour. May the hope go forth that the celebrations will mark a revival in interest in Goethe's work in which students will find stores of practical knowledge too long hidden from the victims of the State.

VI

Lord Acton, A Great European

HISTORY RECORDS MANY EXAMPLES OF STUDENTS GATH-
ering around a teacher whose influence is so profound
that in later life the young men confess that their
careers have been shaped by the lectures to which they
have listened. Perhaps one of the most striking instances
of this was Abélard in the twelfth century. Even after
he was accused of historical heresy and suffered great
persecution, scores of students flocked to hear him.
When he sought a solitary domain in which to build a
rude cabin of wattle, suitable for a hermit, the students
in Paris, learning of his retreat, went in great numbers
and erected hundreds of huts about his simple abode.
Such is the story of Abélard.

There were many others in medieval days to whom
the young people went in throngs to hear something of
the philosophy of culture. This desire to be instructed
by a master was one of the most hopeful manifestations
of youth. Once the student was convinced that his preceptor was a man of knowledge and ready to impart it to
his hearers, the bond was forged which lasted all
through life, and the attachment of pupil to master is
recorded in many works left by those who were so
fortunate as to be members of the group. Some of the
memoirs of famous men refer to their days at college or
university, when they enjoyed the hours spent at lectures
given by a great teacher.

Perhaps one of the most prominent of these was
Lord Acton, who became Regius Professor of History

at the University of Cambridge. But long before he came into direct touch with the students, he had earned for himself an exceptional reputation in the society of studious men; for his learning was encyclopedic, and culturally he was among the few outstanding Europeans whose fame was acknowledged far beyond the borders of his native land. Acton spoke several languages fluently, and frequently took a leading part in many of the profound religious and political controversies of the continent of Europe. Indeed, he was the perfect type of a European.

Born in Naples in 1834, he lived sixty-eight years full of intellectual and cultural activity in many lands. His first school was St. Mary's College, Oscott, where, in addition to Latin and Greek, he set himself the task of learning Spanish, Irish, and Chinese at the age of eleven. His masters were ripe scholars. The president of Oscott was Dr. Wiseman, afterwards the famous cardinal, and two of his instructors were J. B. Morris, a Fellow of Exeter, and Dr. Spencer Logan. Years afterwards, when Wilfred Ward was writing his life of Wiseman, Acton said in a letter to him: "We used to see him [Wiseman] with Lord Shrewsbury, with O'Connell, with Father Mathew, with a Mesopotamian patriarch, with Newman, with Pugin, and we had a feeling that Oscott, next to Pekin, was the centre of the world."

It is almost unbelievable that this young man was refused admission as an undergraduate at Cambridge University because he was a Catholic. The question then arose as to where he should go to resume his education. When this crisis presented itself, he turned to his mother, who had become the wife of Lord Granville, and she, having met Dr. Döllinger at Tegernsee, the country estate of Count Arco-Valley, her brother-in-law, suggested that her son should go to Munich.

Thus began one of the most interesting educational associations of modern days. Döllinger possessed a towering intellect. He was known wherever scholars gathered. Of him the *Dublin Review* said:

> There is hardly a book, old or new, in the different nations of Europe that he has not read, or at least consulted; even the most recent publication, if it stands in the slightest relation to the object of his inquiry, is not overlooked.

As things turned out, it was not unfortunate that Acton was debarred from the English universities because of his religion, for Munich in the middle of the last century was the cultural center of middle Europe. In some respects it was like Vienna, for it was a pivot upon which those from east and west paused for a time to enjoy the marvelous development undertaken by Maximilian. The Royal Library contained more than 1,300,000 printed volumes and no less than 30,000 manuscripts. Besides, there were galleries of wonderful paintings and sculpture. The Court Opera and the Residenz-Theater were famous for the productions of opera and drama. Munich was, indeed, the perfect school for such a pupil as Acton.

However, it is curious that he has left us little in his writings about the cultural advantages of the city in which he spent some of his most impressionable years. Stranger still, we find very few references to the county in which his estate lay in England.

Aldenham Hall, the home of Lord Acton, stood near Bridgnorth in one of the loveliest parts of Shropshire. It was far enough removed from such towns as Kidderminster and Wolverhampton, on the edge of the Black Country, to bask in the pure air of a rich agricultural district. The Severn flowed beneath the walls of the old town, and not far away was Acton Burnell, where Edward I held the Parliament in 1283. The Acton family was an old one, and its members have always been regarded as "proud Salopians."

Perhaps no county in England is the repository of remains so expressive of the thought of Lord Acton as

that of his forebears. Within a short distance of Bridgnorth, on the Severn, lie the ruins of the abbeys of
Lilleshall, Buildwas, and Wenlock. Farther to the
northwest, in the direction of Shrewsbury, there are
the vestiges of the Roman town of Uriconium. Indeed,
it may be said that this country contains the evidence of
the growth of Church and State since Mercian days.
The old saying that Salop is a book of history that can
be read by anyone who rambles about, and has the mind
to learn "summat about what he sees," is near the mark.
Yet, Acton left us few observations on the history of
the county in which his estate lay.

It was at Aldenham Hall that he collected his famous
library which was bought by Andrew Carnegie and afterwards donated by John Morley to Cambridge University.
This is one of the priceless possessions gathered together
by one man. He began the work of collection when he
was with Döllinger at Munich. It contains nearly 60,000
volumes and most of them reveal the work of the student
by the comments in the margins, to say nothing of the
pages that are interleaved and covered with notes.

His stepfather, Lord Granville, wrote from Aldenham
to Lord Canning:

> . . . His library is becoming immense. He has remodelled the
> old library. He has entirely filled the hall; he has furnished
> his own room with books, and he has bagged a bedroom for
> the same purpose. I can hardly open a book without finding
> notes or marks of his . . . .

It is not often that a pupil succeeds in attaining an
excellence comparable to that of such a master as
Döllinger. In this respect Acton is somewhat unique,
for as a young man in the early thirties his learning
was acknowledged by many of the leading men of that
time. Of course he had opportunities that were denied
to his preceptor. In Italy, Germany, France, and England, owing to his family associations, he was welcomed
in the circles of society where he met those who were

then famous in religious and political affairs. A list of names of the well-known people with whom he was acquainted during that period would run into the hundreds. The observations of an admirer that Acton knew everything worth knowing and everybody of importance was an exaggeration, but such a one as gives us an indication of his prestige. Moreover, he was a learned man who loved life and entered into the spirit of the sane social gatherings of the capitals with the address of a courtier and the polish of a wit. His erudition did not weigh so heavily upon him that he could not rise to the occasion and enter cheerfully into the harmless gossip of the moment. Herbert Paul, in his introductory memoir to *Lord Acton's Letters to Mary Gladstone*, tells us that he was a *bon vivant*, a thorough man of the world, and that he was an excellent judge of cooking and of wine. Yet, this man who fought against ultramontanism and the Vatican was a passionate believer in the Church.

From Döllinger Acton learned the thorough rudiments of the historical method, which he pursued all through his life. In his search for truth he never hesitated to denounce what he firmly believed to be untrue in history and sinful in politicians and priests.

It is surprising now to find a revival of interest in him because his thought is so far removed from that of our religious and political schools. He was concerned with fundamentals and would have abhorred most of the nostrums that are served today as the wisdom of an age of progress culminating in the atomic bomb. It is also strange that there is a renewal of interest in his essays, for there is nothing in them that could countenance the bureaucratic recklessness and the regimentation of man, which are the most noticeable features of the times in which we live. The superficiality of political thought and the corruption which is now an everyday affair in politics would have driven Acton into solitude. The faith that he revealed in the Essays on Freedom, concerning a moral system that free men could enjoy,

would have been shattered completely. We have only to
turn to the Letters that he wrote to Mary Gladstone to
discover the real man and understand his wide interests
and the depth of his mind. Where he went, the people
he met, the subjects discussed, taken together with
what he was thinking, what he was reading, and the
plans that he was making, particularly about his
History of Freedom, which was not written, present a
rare person—one with enduring faith in man as a
thinking being.

There is life in these Letters, and the student who
would take up the essays should read them as a pre-
paratory course for the understanding of their author.
There is not a dull line in them, and for an exposition
of intellectual honesty, they are as stimulating as any
that have been published.

We might now turn to the works and learn from this
many-sided man what he thought about the political
conditions of his day. This should be of great interest
to the student because the opinions expresssed therein
are those of one who was intimately associated with the
leading politicians of Europe and America. He abomi-
nated the time-serving demagogue who battens upon
the taxpayer, and he abhorred historians who refused
to record facts that were unfavorable to the State and
its ministers. When he reviewed Phillimore's *History of
England*, he said:

> It is certainly most desirable that something should be
> written that would abate the conceit and self-satisfaction
> with which we Englishmen contemplate ourselves. Many
> of the qualities we prize most highly in theory are those
> which appear least visibly in our history. No Christian annals
> are so sanguinary as ours . . . .

It is well for us to remember such pronouncements
and to understand that it was not Acton alone who
recognized this fact; similar statements had been made
by John Bright and Richard Cobden. However, the

English skin at that time was not so easily scratched as it is today.

No one had a better appreciation than Acton of the utility of government and the extent of its powers. In a few lines he put this in a nutshell:

> *The true distinction between despotism and constitutional government does not lie in the limitation of power but in the existence of means for making power accountable for its behaviour.*

And so keen was his sense of the purpose and aim of political liberty that he did not cease to keep this in view and repeat it many times in his essays:

> Liberty is not a means to a higher political end. It is itself the highest political end. It is not for the sake of a good political administration that it is required, but for security in pursuit of the objects of civil society and private life.

And how true is the following:

> . . . Liberty deteriorates unless it has to struggle for its own existence; and struggle it must, inevitably, and recurrently; for *the passion for power over others can never cease to threaten mankind* . . . .

This seems like an echo of the warnings of our Founding Fathers. Alas, they have fallen upon deaf ears! There is no struggle today to conserve that which was the dominant desire of the Revolutionists.

No one during his period realized so well as he the clear intentions of the men who made this country a Republic.

> . . . It was from America that the plain ideas that men ought to mind their own business, and that the nation is responsible to Heaven for the acts of the State, ideas long locked in the breast of solitary thinkers and hidden away in Latin folios, burst forth like a conqueror upon the world they were destined to transform under the title of the Rights of Man.

Who, in politics today, minds his own business? And it might be asked: Who likes the cost of interfering

with the business of others? But politics, as viewed by
Acton, was something far higher than the practice we
have become used to since we departed from the custom
of letting the people themselves settle their own troubles. Of course, it should be remembered that Acton
lived in the days of what was called "splendid isola-
tion." He would have been called a Nazi if he had
lived in our day and gave voice to his opinions. Still,
he was in the true line of descent from the British
Whigs. He wrote to Mary Gladstone, saying: "I know I
am much more favourable to the great Whig connection,
to the tradition of Locke and Somers, Adam Smith and
Burke and Macaulay, than Mr. Gladstone would like."

And this was written in opposition to his suspicion of
early impressions and of doctrines unaccounted for. He
would have agreed, no doubt, with George Savile
(Marquis of Halifax) who said, "Religion is the foundation of government; without it man is an abandoned
creature, one of the worst beasts Nature hath produced."

Acton's faith in true democracy remained steadfast,
and his belief in its future seems to us today strange and
out of place. But at that time many of the great thinkers
of Europe, in France and in Germany, imagined that
education would not tend to deprive men of their
religious ideas, for it was thought that the spread of
knowledge would enlighten men and help them to
rise to better things. He wrote to Mary Gladstone:

> The generation you consult will be more democratic and
> better instructed than our own; for the progress of democracy,
> though not constant, is certain, and the progress of knowl-
> edge is both constant and certain. It will be more severe in
> literary judgments, and more generous in political.

Surely such a hope as this must remind us how far
we have departed from the aim of many men who lived
before the great wars that began in this century. Such a
statement made about seventy years ago marks the
amazing changes that have wrought havoc with the

hopes of those who placed their faith in education as
an instrument of enlightenment. Still, we may be living
in one of the inconstant periods when democracy is in
need of new rims for its wheels and has been shunted
down a siding for repairs. The prospect of getting it on
to the main line again is not a hopeful one, for knowledge of its usefulness is disclaimed by those who have
abused it and imagine a bureaucracy is better suited to
an ignorant electorate.

Acton would not have lifted his hand to save a shred
of what we now call democracy. His thought was so
far removed from that of the illiterate mob that they
would not have known the figure of democracy that he
respected. In all probability, she would have been
stoned by our so-called democrats.

Gladstone's definition—"trust in the people, tempered
by prudence"—appealed to Acton, and that was the
Liberal understanding of the term during his lifetime.

In reviewing Sir Erskine May's *Democracy in Europe*,
he wrote: "Democracy, like monarchy, is salutary
within limits and fatal in excess; . . . it is the truest
friend of freedom or its most unrelenting foe."

A democracy that countenances graft, dole, and
regimentation, could not have been imagined by the
Liberals of the middle of the last century. And as for
one sanctioning military ascendancy in the government
by imposing upon men the rule of drill and drum, it
could not have been thought of, for it was the Liberal
creed at the time to live in peace with one's neighbors.
Yet, Acton often seems to be conscious of the political
pitfalls set for the unwary: "A true Liberal," he says,
"as distinguished from a Democrat, keeps this peril
always before him." And he was convinced that "there
is no error so monstrous that it fails to find defenders
among the ablest men."

In recent articles and reviews on Acton and his work,
the following well-known declaration has been quoted—

"Power tends to corrupt, and absolute power corrupts absolutely." Snipped from its context, it loses its force and seems rather bald although the statement is emphatic. In the controversy that arose over Acton's article in the *English Historical Review* on the "History of the Papacy," Mandell Creighton, the editor of the volumes, took issue with the writer, and in one of the most powerful letters that Acton ever wrote, he defended his position. Strange to say, this defense of the position which Acton took has not been revealed, but it is to be found among his letters to Bishop Creighton and has been reproduced in part in the Appendix to the *Historical Essays and Studies*, published in 1907. Every word he wrote to Creighton is worth remembering, for in this generation drawing to a close, we have had, unhappily, so many examples of the power which tends to corrupt that the words of Acton are as timely now as they were when the article was written in 1887. There is room only to quote the following excerpt:

> . . . I cannot accept your canon that we are to judge Pope and King unlike other men, with a favourable presumption that they did no wrong. If there is any presumption it is the other way, against the holders of power, increasing as the power increases. Historic responsibility has to make up for the want of legal responsibility. Power tends to corrupt, and absolute power corrupts absolutely. Great men are almost always bad men, even when they exercise influence and not authority, still more when you superadd the tendency or the certainty of corruption by authority. There is no worse heresy than that the office sanctifies the holder of it. That is the point at which the negation of Catholicism and the negation of Liberalism meet and keep high festival, and the end learns to justify the means. You would hang a man of no position like Ravaillac; but if what one hears is true, then Elizabeth asked the gaoler to murder Mary, and William III ordered his Scots minister to extirpate a clan. Here are the greatest names coupled with the greatest crimes; you would spare those criminals, for some mysterious reason. I would hang them higher than Haman, for reasons of quite obvious justice, still more, still higher for the sake of historical science.

Here is a text which should be hung on the portals of our schools: "The law of liberty tends to abolish the reign of race over race, of faith over faith, of class over class." We ought to take the following to heart at this time, for many an honest man might write it today in connection with the scandals reported on the front pages of our journals:

> . . . We deal only with responsibility for public acts. But with these we must deal freely. We have to keep the national conscience straight and true, and if we shrink from doing this because we dare not cast obloquy on class or party or institution, then we become accomplices in wrong-doing, and very possibly in crime.

How John Morley, when he wrote the *Life of Gladstone*, could miss the importance of Acton's association with Gladstone is difficult to explain. Matthew Arnold said: "Gladstone influences all around him, but Acton: it is Acton who influences Gladstone."

I do not know of anyone who studied the Grand Old Man so closely and so deeply as Acton did. This should be clear to those who will read that extraordinary letter to Mary Gladstone, dated Cannes, December 14, 1880, in which Acton devotes many pages to her father's gifts. In this illuminating communication there are many passages that should be preserved because they are of historical value. There is space to mention only one or two. Referring to Gladstone's "science of statesmanship," Acton says:

> The decisive test of his greatness will be the gap he will leave. Among those who come after him there will be none who understand that the men who pay wages ought not to be the political masters of those who earn them, (because laws should be adapted to those who have the heaviest stake in the country, for whom misgovernment means not mortified pride or stinted luxury, but want and pain, and degradation and risk to their own lives and to their children's souls), and who yet can understand and feel sympathy for institutions that incorporate tradition and prolong the reign of the dead.

It might be said that the gap was felt before he died. For he was the one man, had he not retired, who could have opposed the South African policy of Chamberlain and Rhodes with a chance of success. Another passage from this letter should be recorded, for what it states is very well worth deep consideration at this time:

> . . . We know that the doctrine of equality leads by steps not only logical, but almost mechanical, to sacrifice the principle of liberty to the principle of quantity; that, being unable to abdicate responsibility and power, it attacks genuine representation, and, as there is no limit where there is no control, invades, sooner or later, both property and religion.

In discussing the propositions of Adam Smith concerning the contracts between labor and capital, Acton declares:

> . . . If there is a free contract, in open market, between capital and labour, it cannot be right that one of the two contracting parties should have the making of the laws, the management of the conditions, the keeping of the peace, the administration of justice, the distribution of taxes, the control of expenditure, in its own hands exclusively. It is unjust that all these securities, all these advantages, should be on the same side. It is monstrous that they should be all on the side that has least urgent need of them, that has least to lose . . .

This from a nobleman and a landlord is refreshing and reminds one of the notions held by Francis Place, the pioneer who was responsible for the reform of labor conditions more than a generation before Acton wrote. In a letter dated February 7, 1824, Place said: "Leave workmen and their employers as much as possible at liberty to make their own bargains in their own way."

And now we must turn to some of Acton's thoughts on history and historians. It should be remembered that at that time in England there were such outstanding jurists as Sir Henry Maine, Sir Frederick Pollock, and Frederic William Maitland—eminent historians who have left indispensable works. Maitland was recognized as one of the most learned men at the University of Cambridge. In referring to Acton's erudition he said: "If we recall the giants of a past time, their wondrous memories, their encyclopedic knowledge, we must remember also how much that Lord Acton knew was for them practically unknowable."

Maitland also tells us how Acton toiled "in the archives hunting the little fact that makes the difference." Early in his life Acton realized that "no part of modern history has been so searched and sifted as to be without urgent need of new and deeper inquiry, and the touch of a fresh mind." And he was convinced that "all understanding of history depends on one's understanding the forces that make it, of which religious forces are the most active and the most definite."

He was conscious, too, that ideas play a more important part in historical crises than many writers imagine. On this point he says, "the great object, in trying to understand history, political, religious, literary or scientific, is to get behind men and to grasp ideas."

I do not know where we should look for a finer exposition of the true approach to history than that which is contained in the "Inaugural Lecture on the Study of History," delivered at Cambridge, in June, 1895. The reader of this masterly address should remember that it was given more than sixty years ago, when there was a sense of liberty in the universities which permitted full freedom of thought and speech. The vast scope of his erudition was devoted to the preparation of the lecture, and I am glad it has been incorporated in *Essays on Freedom and Power*, by Lord Acton, issued by The Beacon Press (1948). In the 1906 edition of *Lectures on Modern History*, there is an Appendix of notes covering twenty-three pages of small print and dealing with 105 items. It will come as a shock to the specialist who treats exclusively of a dynasty, or a political upheaval, or the character of a statesman to learn how Acton approached his problem:

You have often heard it said that Modern History is a subject to which neither beginning nor end can be assigned. No beginning, because the dense web of the fortunes of man is woven without a void; because, in society as in nature, the structure is continuous, and we can trace things back uninterruptedly, until we dimly descry the Declaration of Independence in the forests of Germany. No end, because, on the same principle, history made and history making are scientifically inseparable and separately unmeaning.

Those who have taken snippets of history in some of the courses prescribed in our schools may be surprised to learn from this lecture that the present can only be understood by those who have a knowledge of the past. Acton says, "If the past has been an obstacle and a burden, knowledge of the past is the safest and surest emancipation." There are so many surprises in this address for our students that many will wonder why they have not been introduced to it before this. Here is one: "No intellectual exercise can be more invigorating than to watch the working of the mind of Napoleon, the most entirely known as well as the ablest of historic men."

When, on fuller knowledge, we re-examine the histories of many of our political and religious heroes we find them lacking in the virtues claimed for them by their biographers, and Acton pointed this out in his review of Tocqueville's *Souvenirs*:

We cannot form a judgment until we know the worst of the cause to be tried. From the time when the biographical element becomes distinct, for the last five hundred years, there is this constant result, that fewer characters bear the searchlight; and it may generally be affirmed of ruling and leading spirits that, the better we know them, the worse they appear.

What is the real purpose of research that should guide the investigator, when he begins to examine the records of the past? Acton in a letter to Mary Gladstone gives us a hint of how we should proceed:

> . . . What we want to know is why the old world that had
> lasted so long went to ruin, how the doctrine of equality
> sprang into omnipotence, how it changed the principles of
> administration, justice, international law, taxation, represen-
> tation, property, and religion . . . .

Modern History has had a long beginning, and if we
are to understand how we have reached the present
stage, it is necessary to review, as Acton did, the
amazing changes that shook the world after the discovery of America. For him, Modern History began
about the close of the fifteenth century:

> . . . When Columbus subverted the notions of the world, and
> reversed the conditions of production, wealth, and power;
> Machiavelli released Government from the restraint of law;
> Erasmus diverted the current of ancient learning from profane
> into Christian channels; Luther broke the chain of authority
> and tradition at the strongest link; and Copernicus erected an
> invincible power that set for ever the mark of progress upon
> the time that was to come.

Dr. Henry Jackson who knew Acton said, ''History,
as he conceived it, included in its scope all forms of
human activity; so that scholars, whom others would
describe as theologians or jurists were in his eyes great
departmental historians.''

In the postscript of a letter to Bishop Creighton he
gave

ADVICE TO PERSONS ABOUT TO WRITE HISTORY—DON'T

In the Moral Sciences Prejudice is Dishonesty.

A Historian has to fight against temptations special to his
mode of life, temptations from Country, Class, Church,
College, Party, Authority of talents, solicitation of friends.

The most respectable of these influences are the most dangerous.

The historian who neglects to root them out is exactly
like a juror who votes according to his personal likes or
dislikes.

In judging men and things Ethics go before Dogma,
Politics or Nationality. The Ethics of History cannot be
denominational. . . .

The list of subjects treated in the first two volumes of the *Essays* covers nearly all the most important epochs and crises in the history of Europe and America. It is impossible to put a just estimate upon the erudition of Acton, but a student of history will be well repaid to take the essays edited by Dr. J. N. Figgis and Professor R. V. Laurence (both lecturers at Cambridge) and give them deep consideration, if he has the slightest desire to appreciate the invaluable work to which Acton devoted his career. Moreover, an interested reader will find excitement in the new interpretation and in the vast number of emendations of old notions, which appear on nearly every other page. A thorough reading of the contents of the three volumes will go far toward making an informed man of one who undertakes the task. It is amazing to find students and instructors wasting time on ephemeral studies when they might be delving into such mines of information as can be found in Acton's works.

VII

Lord Acton as a Critic

THOSE WHO ARE PLANNING A CAREER IN THE FIELD OF historical literature cannot afford to overlook the aids given so abundantly by Lord Acton in his reviews of books. Scholars of twenty years ago frequently pointed out examples of literary criticism from his pen which were of exceptional value. His essay on the "Introduction to L. A. Burd's Edition of *Il Principe* by Machiavelli" has been selected several times as a unique specimen of critical achievement.

In many respects it is a review of the opinions of writers who have dealt with *The Prince* or have been influenced by its State creed. To enjoy it thoroughly, the reader should be a master of five or six languages or have the passages translated for him by a scholar. This writer was fortunate enough to have a friend who had no difficulty in doing this. Nevertheless, it is possible to read it without translating all the passages, for Acton sustains the interest in his own language; and one is never at a loss in following the direction of his opinion. The chief reason why Acton's review of Burd's Edition is referred to here is that we should be reminded of the ideas of Machiavelli. The principles he formulated for the State have not fallen into desuetude, but are as vital today to its strength as they were to the rulers of Florence and Venice. Acton points this clearly:

> Among these utterances of capable and distinguished men, it will be seen that some are partially true, and others, without a particle of truth, are at least representative and signifi-

cant, and serve to bring Machiavelli within fathomable depth. He is the earliest conscious and articulate exponent of certain living forces in the present world. Religion, progressive enlightenment, the perpetual vigilance of public opinion, have not reduced his empire, or disproved the justice of his conception of mankind. He obtains a new lease of life from causes that are still prevailing, and from doctrines that are apparent in politics, philosophy, and science. Without sparing censure, or employing for comparison the grosser symptoms of the age, we find him near our common level, and perceive that he is not a vanishing type, but a constant and contemporary influence. Where it is impossible to praise, to defend, or to excuse, the burden of blame may yet be lightened by adjustment and distribution, and he is more rationally intelligible when illustrated by lights falling not only from the century he wrote in, but from our own, which has seen the course of its history twenty-five times diverted by actual or attempted crime.

Had Acton lived through the two wars that have blighted this century, he would undoubtedly have marked the influence of the famous Florentine at work in the nationalistic policies of the powers.

Another review of particular value to us is that on *The American Commonwealth*, by James Bryce. The lecture that he delivered at the Literary and Scientific Institution, Bridgnorth, 1866, on "The Civil War in America" is also of unusual interest to our readers, for it contains an appraisal of the termination of the conflict that we might consider deeply at this time:

> It is a noble sight to see this mighty soldier [Lee], the greatest of the countrymen of Washington, exhorting his people to obey their conquerors, and giving the example of peaceful retirement and submission. But it is also a noble sight to see the chief of a mighty and victorious nation . . . staying the hand of vengeance, remitting punishment and disbanding armies, and treating as an equal the man who had been so lately and so long the most terrible of enemies, and whose splendid talents had inflicted on the people of the Union a gigantic loss in treasure, blood, and fame. It is too soon to despair of a community that has among its leading citizens such men as these.

Whether the men of today are less fitted to make
terms of peace, on which a future of amity may be built,
than those of Lincoln's day may be inferred from such a
tribute as Acton paid to Grant and Lee. Then the
atrocities of war were overlooked, as the angel of
peace spread her wings over the fields saturated with the
blood of heroic men who obeyed their commanders.
The main object of those who had been engaged in the
conflict seemed to be to leave no gaping wounds of
hate behind them, if they could do anything to salve
them. How different it has been with warring States in
our time and generation! What reversions of thought
and practice have taken place! If a reading of Acton's
essays and reviews had no other purpose than that of
reminding us of these changes, they would merit the
profound consideration of people who desire peace. He
said, "The reward of history is that it releases and
relieves us from present strife."

So far, we have not enjoyed this reward, and there
seems to be little chance of our doing so. Perhaps we
shall have to find another definition for barbarism, for
nothing that went by that name in the past is comparable to what has occurred during the last ten years.

Not a few of the books that have been given to us as
history, written since the end of the First World War,
will suffer severely at the hands of a future Acton, if
the next generation is so fortunate as to be blessed with
one. The sins of writers on serious subjects, which he
made it his duty to expose, were never so prevalent as
they are today. But the printing presses serving publishers and journalists have simpler means for reaching
the multitude; and the radio, a device for distorting
the public mind by time-serving propagandists has
wrought irreparable damage upon the minds of people.
In recent months we have witnessed several examples
of the difficulties of publication encountered by writers
who oppose the popular trends. There is a censorship

in force today which, in some respects, is as strict as that we suffered during the war. Persons and policies must not be questioned, and it is just as hard to get at secret documents in the archives of government offices as it was to get into the cupboards of the Quai d'Orsay for information after World War I. It seems strange now to read the advice that was given to the students at Cambridge when Acton delivered his "Inaugural Lecture on the Study of History." He said:

> . . . For our purpose, the main thing to learn is not the art of accumulating material, but the sublimer art of investigating it, of discerning truth from falsehood and certainty from doubt. It is by solidity of criticism more than by the plenitude of erudition, that the study of history strengthens, and straightens, and extends the mind. And the accession of the critic in the place of the indefatigable compiler, of the artist in coloured narrative, the skilled limner of character, the persuasive advocate of good, or other, causes, amounts to a transfer of government, to a change of dynasty, in the historic realm. For the critic is one who, when he lights on an interesting statement, begins by suspecting it. He remains in suspense until he has subjected his authority to three operations. First, he asks whether he has read the passage as the author wrote it. For the transcriber, and the editor, and the official or officious censor on the top of the editor, have played strange tricks, and have much to answer for. And if they are not to blame, it may turn out that the author wrote his book twice over, that you can discover the first jet, the progressive variations, things added, and things struck out. Next is the question where the writer got his information. If from a previous writer, it can be ascertained, and the inquiry has to be repeated. If from unpublished papers, they must be traced, and when the fountain-head is reached, or the track disappears, the question of veracity arises. The responsible writer's character, his position, antecedents, and probable motives have to be examined into; and this is what, in a different and adapted sense of the word, may be called the higher criticism, in comparison with the servile and often mechanical work of pursuing statements to their root. For a historian has to be treated as a witness, and not believed unless his sincerity is established. The maxim that a man must be presumed to be innocent until his guilt is proved, was not made for him.

Professors of history who have undertaken the responsibility of teaching our youths the canons of historical method might spend time on Acton and impart to their pupils some of the great principles that he laid down. The suffocating air of the classrooms, of which so many complain, might be dispersed; and if the windows of enlightenment were thrown open to let in the air he breathed, historical writing, within a generation, might flourish as he believed it would.

It is not only the depth of Acton's learning that is revealed in his literary criticisms, but also the keen desire to hold the balance fairly between the opposing forces and give judgment in a spirit of understanding the issues. With all his severity expressed against error, he weighed the acts and consequences impartially, without a tinge of prejudice.

When the novel, *John Inglesant*, appeared, it created something of a sensation. The author, John Henry Shorthouse, was a Birmingham chemical manufacturer. He came from a Quaker family, but on reaching manhood, was baptized into the Church of England. Eighty thousand copies of the work were sold. In the most unlikely quarters, it made people think, and it was discussed widely in intellectual circles. All who were concerned in the eternal conflict between the flesh and the spirit debated the merits of this book for a long time. In a letter to Mary Gladstone, Acton wrote:

> Wickham lent me John Inglesant yesterday, and I finished it before bedtime. I have read nothing more thoughtful and suggestive since Middlemarch, and I could fill with honest praise the pages I am going to blacken with complaint. But if I had access to the author, with privilege of free and indiscreet speech, it would seem a worthier tribute to his temper and ability to lay my litany of doubts before him. Not having it, I submit my questionings to yourself, as the warmest admirer of his work.

Then for fourteen pages we read one of the most extraordinary reviews of a serious novel that has ever

been published. He not only points out the errors in
the work as to names, periods, and occurrences, but he
supplies the information the author did not possess.
This should be a compulsory study for any young man
fitting himself for a career in literature of the higher
order. The chief complaints that Acton makes are
concerned with the historical errors. It might be well
to quote one paragraph which gives a sample of Acton's
method, and in which he reveals the high standard
that he placed upon historical accuracy:

> The Jesuit who is so hopeful of Anglican reunion that
> he will not allow his favourite pupil to join the Church of
> Rome is called Sancta Clara. There was a Father Sancta Clara
> in those days, who is peculiarly well remembered among Eng-
> lish Catholics as the greatest writer we had between Staple-
> ton and Newman, less acute than the one, less eloquent than
> the other, more learned than either; remarkable for opinions
> so conciliatory as to resemble those of his imaginary name-
> sake, and to make him the originator and suggester of No.
> XC. [an Oxford Tract]; remarkable also for the extreme
> difficulty of getting his books. But he was a Franciscan, not a
> Jesuit, a scholar, not an intriguer; and his name was not
> Hall, but Davenport.

If the practice of taking pains be an attribute of genius,
Acton had it in good measure. In the criticism of *John
Inglesant* there is clear evidence of the speed and thor-
oughness of a skilled workman. The feat of reading a
long novel and writing a review of it was accomplished
within forty-eight hours. Such a performance gives one
an idea of how Acton devoured books—a wonder that
puzzled many who came under his spell. We can present
no better example of the value of having an immense
background of knowledge in literature, for he seems
never to have been at a loss to verify a statement and,
furthermore, none of the essays reveals the slightest
uncertainty in his attack upon the errors of an author.
He seemed to be at home in any period and to be familiar
with the personages who ruled, and their courtiers also,

whether they were at St. Peter's, at Westminster, or at the Louvre.

The scope of the *Historical Essays and Studies*, which deal with "Wolsey and the Divorce of Henry VIII," "The Rise and Fall of the Mexican Empire," "German Schools of History," "A History of the Papacy," "Mabillon," and many others, forms a towering monument of knowledge which, for grandeur of thought, will never be surpassed.

As a critic, Acton has been accused of severity and ruthlessness, and there may be some truth in this. But when it is realized how high the standard was that he set for himself, no one should take exception to it. Who would wrest from him the rod he used figuratively upon the backs of the writers who blundered? Some of the wittiest passages we have in our language may be found in the castigations he administered. Dealing with M. Laurent, he remarks that:

> sometimes it even happens that his information is not secondhand, and there are some original authorities with which he is evidently familiar. The ardour of his opinions, so different from those which have usually distorted history, gives an interest even to his grossest errors.

Why should he spare a careless author? He was never known to spare himself. In literature, mercy cannot be extended to stupidity. As a judge of men and their actions in and out of Church and State, he was supreme. Consider the following gem:

> Lord Liverpool governed England in the present crisis of the war, and for twelve troubled years of peace, chosen not by the nation, but by the owners of the land. The English gentry were well content with an order of things by which for a century and a quarter they had enjoyed so much prosperity and power. Desiring no change they wished for no ideas. They sympathised with the complacent respectability of Lord Liverpool's character, and knew how to value the safe sterility of his mind. He distanced statesmen like Grenville, Wellesley, and Canning, not in spite of his inferiority, but by

reason of it. His mediocrity was his merit. The secret of his
policy was that he had none. For six years his administration
outdid the Holy Alliance. For five years it led the liberal
movement throughout the world. The Prime Minister
hardly knew the difference. He it was who forced Canning
on the King. In the same spirit he wished his government to
include men who were in favour of the Catholic claims and
men who were opposed to them. His career exemplifies, not
the accidental combination but the natural affinity, between
the love of conservatism and the fear of ideas.

Lord Acton, however, held an essential degree of
rectitude for himself in dealing with the works of his
day by exercising an assiduous care for the public mind
which might be led astray by popular reviewers of a
book that attracted attention. He wrote two articles
for *The Rambler* on Buckle's *History of Civilization in
England*. After showing clearly the many errors of
which Buckle was guilty, Acton remarks:

> . . . We have said quite enough to show that Mr. Buckle's
> learning is as false as his theory, and that the ostentation of
> his slovenly erudition is but an artifice of ignorance. In his
> laborious endeavour to degrade the history of mankind, and
> of the dealings of God with man, to the level of one of the
> natural sciences, he has stripped it of its philosophical, of
> its divine, and even of its human character and interest. . . .
> We could not allow a book to pass without notice into general
> circulation and popularity which is written in an impious and
> degrading spirit, redeemed by no superiority or modesty of
> learning, by no earnest love of truth, and by no open dealing
> with opponents.
>
> We may rejoice that the true character of an infidel philos-
> ophy has been brought to light by the monstrous and absurd
> results to which it has led this writer, who has succeeded in
> extending its principles to the history of civilization only at
> the sacrifice of every quality which makes a history great.

His candor was sharp, incisive. He hated a sham,
and he knew that it was easy for a so-called bigwig to
shine in the company of bald-headed minds. Yet, no
one was ever so open and generous to those who desired
knowledge. He seemed to be ready at all times to lend

the stores of his mind and his library to those who sought information. There is no record of anyone who appealed to him being turned away unsatisfied.

The intellectual caliber of Acton appears in many of his reviews, but there is none that shows it so brilliantly as the one on "George Eliot's Life." She is now forgotten, but she had a great influence on the English people while Acton was at work. Her atheism did not preclude her from his consideration. Perhaps no one has given such proof of the realization of her genius as we find in this essay and in the *Letters to Mary Gladstone*. Coming from such a source, what could be finer than the following:

> . . . She thought that the world would be indefinitely better and happier if man could be made to feel that there is no escape from the inexorable law that we reap what we have sown.

and

> . . . There will be more perfect novels and truer systems. But she has little rivalry to apprehend until philosophy inspires finer novels, or novelists teach nobler lessons of duty to the masses of men. If ever science or religion reigns alone over an undivided empire, the books of George Eliot might lose their central and unique importance, but as the emblem of a generation distracted between the intense need of believing and the difficulty of belief, they will live to the last syllable of recorded time.

In these days when we are served in history with the work of the specialist, it is almost an educational duty for the man who wishes to be informed and to acquire a large view of the religious and political events of the centuries, to turn back to these essays and enjoy the treasures they contain. It is sad to think how few of our libraries have Lord Acton's books upon their shelves. Several years ago, two American universities of high standing contained only one volume apiece: the *History of Freedom* and the *Lectures on Modern History*

respectively. When, about 1927, I lectured at a university
on "Freedom in Antiquity" and "Freedom in Christianity," I was amazed to find only one man at the
gathering who had read a volume of Acton.

And, yet, there was never greater need for his knowledge and wisdom. Most of the mistakes we have made
in the past two generations have arisen from our unut-
terable ignorance of European affairs. The politicians in
Great Britain and in this country have shown either
that they have not understood the history of Europe,
or that they have deliberately ignored it.

It cannot be said that Stanley Baldwin or Neville
Chamberlain knew Europe, and who would claim that
Roosevelt or Hull was familiar with her history? The
men at the head of affairs since the First World War
(including the totalitarians of all descriptions) were
nationalists pure and simple, and were unable to direct
their policies toward the maintenance of European peace.
During the fifteen years I devoted to politics in Great
Britain, I met not one of her politicians who was
familiar with the Continent as a student or as a traveler
having direct knowledge of her cultural institutions.
Outside the domain of party politics, I was intimate
with several men whom I met frequently in the capitals
of Europe, who could be called Europeans. In *The
Tragedy of Europe* I have made some observations on this
curious failing of British politicians and merchants, and
the shocking neglect they often betrayed of information
that would have given them a clearer understanding of
the issues with which they had to deal. The European
mind cannot very well be cultivated at home in the
midst of national strivings. It has been described by
Jacob Burckhardt as follows:

> The European quality is that by which all human forces
> become articulate, expressing themselves in stone, in images,
> in words, in institutions, and political parties, down to the
> individual. It is the vitalization of everything spiritual in
> every aspect and direction. . . .

Now that we consider ourselves a world power and are going to send our military police to keep order far from our shores, the least we can do is to learn something about the people to be subordinated to our conception of how they should live and think. There is no one who can supply the necessary information as well as Acton.

There is a passage in his essay on "German Schools of History," which reminds me of the many references to Sir Henry Maine to be found in the *Letters to Mary Gladstone*. It is as follows:

> When Germans assert that their real supremacy rests with their historians, they mean it in the sense of Bentley and Colebrooke, not of Machiavelli and Saint-Simon, in the sense in which the Bishop of Durham [Dr. Lightfoot] and Sir Henry Maine take the lead in England, the sense in which M. Fustel de Coulanges calls history the most arduous of the sciences.

Now that Dr. Toynbee has found thousands of readers for his *Study of History*, it is not inappropriate to remind students of the works of Maine. Toynbee seems to have overlooked them, and yet such a master as Acton paid high tribute to the author of *Ancient Law*. He considered him one of three of the finest minds in England, and he told Mary Gladstone that "what pure reason and boundless knowledge can do, without sympathy or throb, Maine can do better than any man in England." How seldom one comes across a reference to him now. Has he been forgotten, entirely overlooked by those historians who write upon the economic problems which affect States? Forty or fifty years ago his works were of deep interest to American students. The subjects dealt with by Maine are just as timely now as when they were written. Indeed, *Village Communities* is a necessary work for those who desire to know the primitive beginnings of a people.

It is impossible to read many pages of Acton's essays and miss the flashes of enlightenment which reveal a

well-stored mind. Who, but Acton, would have divined
the link which bound Kant to Joseph Butler, the old
Bishop of Durham, whose *Analogy of Religion* was one
of the great books that influenced many of the leading
thinkers more than two hundred years ago? Lord
Brougham said it was "the most argumentative and
philosophical defense of Christianity ever submitted to
the world." And Sir James Mackintosh proclaimed it
"the most original and profound work extant in any
language on the philosophy of religion." Acton wrote:

> Kant is the macrocosm of Butler (*Analogy* and *Sermons*).
> From him he got his theory of conscience, which has so
> much influenced political as well as religious thought. His
> most famous saying, on the teaching of conscience within us,
> and the firmament above, is taken straight from Butler. I do
> not despair of convincing German friends that what Butler
> compressed into a crowded and obscure volume is substan-
> tially expanded into the minute and subtle philosophy of his
> successor. Kant stands on the shoulders of the *Analogy* when
> he elevates the probability into a substitute for proof, and
> on those of the *Sermons* when he makes the infallible con-
> science a basis of certainty and the source of the Categorical
> Imperative.

A reference to this is to be found in that very useful
book, *As Lord Acton Says*, edited by Professor F. E.
Lally, and published by Remington Ward, Newport,
R. I. (1942). This work may be highly recommended
to students who would seek an excellent introduction
to Acton's life and work.

There seemed to be no limit to the riches of his
knowledge, and one is amazed at the ease with which
he united thought to thought, and traced the parentage
of ideas from ancient times down to modern days. It is
hard to imagine an activity of daily life that he neglected
Of him it may be said his youth was well spent in
constant study. There were no simple manuals, then,
for the student; the hard way was the only one to be
pursued, and he, with unflagging energy of spirit,

acquired the erudition which made him famous. The following from a letter to Mary Gladstone gives us an idea of the years he spent "in looking for men wise enough to solve the problems that puzzle me."

> . . . I was always associated with men a generation older than myself, most of whom died early—for me—and all of whom impressed me with the same moral, that one must do one's learning and thinking for oneself, without expecting short cuts or relying on other men.

Before closing this sketch, it is advisable to present another side of Acton. In the *Letters to Mary Gladstone* he displays a wit in many of them which is most unusual in a pre-eminent scholar. He tells his correspondent to "remember that one touch of ill nature makes the whole world kin." And of a friend he remarks: "His only artifice is his discretion."

Mr. Gladstone frequently visited Holmbury, the house of Frederick Leveson Gower, who gave fine dinner parties and had a host of friends. Acton observed, "Freddy Leveson has a touching fidelity to monotonous friendships."

How Mary Gladstone must have chuckled when she read: "Please remember I am possessed of a Whig devil, and neither Peel nor Pitt lives in my Valhalla." And in the same letter he wrote, "It is a vice, not a merit, to live for expedients and not for ideas."

What could be neater than to observe that certain actions of politicians are "more parliamentary than statesmanlike?" It would be interesting to learn if Mary Gladstone showed her father all the letters she received from Acton. One wonders if he saw the following: "Many things are better for silence than for speech: others are better for speech than for stationery."

How true of so many people is the point in this: "The Duke of Orleans nearly described my feelings when he spoke, testamentarily, of his religious *flag* and his political *faith*."

Acton's description of a self-possessed lady is hard to beat:

——— is very intelligent, agreeable, amiable, a little complex in design; accurate calculation sometimes resides in the corner of her eye, and she knows how to regulate to a hair's breadth, when she smiles, the thin red line of her lips.

Sometimes in a line or two he makes a pronouncement that startles one. Here are two: In writing of Ruskin, he said, "He is one of the few Englishmen of genius; one of the most perfect masters of our language that ever wrote." And of Origen he remarked, "The ablest writer of early times, who spoke with approval of conspiring for the destruction of tyrants."

The Letters are a revelation of the intrigues and schisms of Gladstone's political career, and in summing up his estimate of Mary's father as a statesman, he declared boldly that it was not his successes that impressed him so much as his failures. Acton's mind was big enough to distinguish the greatness in a genius who fails. Always aloof from the popular clamor and the vaporings of the press, his judgment of men and their policies never swerved.

No one looked down on the arena of parliamentary strife and international discord with a more discerning glance and a better appreciation of the weaknessess and foibles of the protagonists who held the fate of the world in their hands. But the hopes he cherished for enlarging the bounds of freedom, and his faith in an extension of knowledge, as a means of encouraging an understanding of the aspirations of the peoples of Europe, were darkened toward the end of his active life. Yet, who would have dreamed, when he died at Tegernsee, in 1902, that the leading politicians were already deliberating moves on the map of Europe which would destroy the continent that he had known and loved? When one reads the Essays on Freedom, it seems inconceivable that two World Wars have taken place within fifty years of his death.

VIII

Humanism, Yesterday and Today

DURING THE LAST QUARTER OF THE NINETEENTH CENTURY when the British and the American rationalists were expounding their doctrines in political and philosophical arenas, there arose many questions as to what they meant when they used the term "humanism" as it applied to everyday affairs, and what significance it had when the same people linked it up with their notions of the Italian Renaissance. There has recently been so much debate as to what these terms stand for that the young student is somewhat confused when he finds that the humanism, that is, the craze for classical books, which arose at the beginning of the fourteenth century, had a totally different meaning from that which is given to it today. Perhaps the fact that, since the days of Auguste Comte, the term humanism has entered so much into sociological studies explains one of the reasons for this misunderstanding. There is no similarity at all between the humanism of today and that of the period when Petrarch and Boccaccio began to collect books.

It has been said that the Italian poet was the first humanist. Dr. Tilley, who wrote the remarkable essay in *The Cambridge Medieval History* on "The Early Renaissance," tells us that Petrarch "was the first to find in ancient literature a larger measure than elsewhere of that learning and training in virtue which are peculiar to men."

Why he should be named the first humanist because of this discovery it is hard to tell, for nearly a thousand years before his time the Ptolemies—Soter and Philadelphus—had formed the two libraries and museum of Alexandria. Later, in the sixth century, Cassiodorus at Squillace brought together a great collection of works, which has been considered by scholars to be the largest of that day. There were other collectors of books and, no doubt, at the centers of learning in Ireland there must have been libraries of high worth within reach of such an intellectual giant as Erigena. So perhaps there was something more than the study of ancient literature to qualify Petrarch for the honor of being the first humanist. Dr. Tilley tells us: "He found in the pages of Virgil and Horace, of Cicero and Seneca, especially in those of Cicero, a concentration of human aims and aspirations and a guide to human endeavour."

However, before Petrarch came upon the scene, there was Albertino Mussato of Padua who, so Dr. Tilley points out, has been called "the initiator of humanism." But the type of humanism that he initiated is not explained.

The passion for gathering ancient works was not new. And as for "human aims" and "guides to human endeavour," the works of Plato reveal in a striking manner that they were the concern of the Greeks centuries before Philo set to work in Alexandria. Who can read *The Republic, Protagoras* and *The Laws* of Plato, and not be impressed with the inquiry shown in these dialogues about human aims and aspirations? These studies devoted to the affairs of man and the State have become as necessary for the reflections of philosophers as *De Legibus* of Cicero. Petrarch and Boccaccio, however, were not in possession of the Greek originals or Greek literature in general until long after the period of Erigena—an interval of six centuries. The fact that others must have been engaged upon the work to which

the Italians so passionately gave their time is revealed
by Roger Bacon who complained that it was difficult to
procure the works of Aristotle.

There is an interesting essay awaiting an author who
will pursue the study of "human aims and aspirations
as a guide to human endeavour," as this seems to have
been the principal intellectual object of the humanists
of the Italian Renaissance. Such an excursion would
lead him far from Europe. Perhaps to China, where he
would find in Confucius and Mencius the same desires—
to foster the aims and aspirations of man—which animated the Italians at the beginning of the fourteenth
century.

Both these Chinese philosophers devoted themselves
to the task of reformation in man and in the State.
Mencius tells us:

> The world had fallen into decay and right principles had
> disappeared. Perverse discourses and oppressive deeds were
> waxen rife. Ministers murdered their rulers and sons their
> fathers.

It would not be necessary to change a word in this
statement to make it apply to the conditions of Europe
during the fourteenth century.

Another quite different notion of humanism is dealt
with by Dr. Gerald Walsh, Professor of Medieval
Culture at Fordham University. This interesting survey
of those whom he classifies as humanists is called *Medieval Humanism*, but his conception of it is far different
from that of "the cult of antiquity." Dr. Walsh says:
"The root idea of humanism is that everyone has the
right, if not the duty, to seek human happiness in a
human way."

But what is that right? To this question the modern
Church has no reply, although many of the Early
Fathers pronounced one in unmistakable terms. They
knew "the footstool of God" was the source from which

all men draw their sustenance, and every child of the Creator has a right to use it for its needs. St. Chrysostom declared:

> God gave the same earth to be cultivated by all. Since, therefore, His bounty is common, how comes it that you have so many fields and your neighbor not even a clod of earth?

And St. Ambrose proclaimed:

> The soil was given to the rich and poor in common. The pagans hold earth as property. They do blaspheme God.

These saints of the Church were humanists of the first order, for they understood the economic essential of human happiness.

The Italian renaissance was not the only one that arose in Europe. In many respects the movements that blossomed under Charlemagne, in the eighth century, and Alfred, in the ninth, were of a far more practical character than those of the fourteenth century, for the early scholars not only collected books as we know from the records left by Bede and Biscop; they fostered the growth of schools and the study of ancient manuscripts. The instruction issued by Charlemagne to the monks and secular canons urged them "not only to get together children of slaves but also the sons of free men, and take them into their societies." They were to be taught psalms, music, arithmetic and grammar and, besides, the writing of good editions of books. Alcuin, who went to the court of Charlemagne, tells us: "The boys not only read Virgil, but they were encouraged to write Latin verses themselves."

The most interesting story in the early history of Christian humanism concerns the life and work of three great ecclesiastics: Aldhelm, Bede, and Alcuin. They followed one another in a period of one hundred and fifty years, from 635 to 804. The abbeys where these men passed their days were famous for their wonderful libraries. We have accounts of how the works were collected. The catalogue of the library at York is preserved. In it we find the Early Fathers represented by fourteen volumes; ten Greek and Roman authors; six ancient grammarians; and six Latin poets. When Alcuin went to the Palace School of Charlemagne, he desired copies of the books he had left at York, and he made the following request:

> If it shall please your wisdom, I will send some of our boys, who may copy from thence whatever is necessary, and carry back into France the flowers of Britain; that the garden may not be shut up in York, but the fruits of it may be placed in the Paradise of Tours.

Professor Christian Pfister of the Sorbonne, a profound student of this period says:

> These letters [Alcuin's], of which 311 are extant, are filled chiefly with pious meditations, but they further form a mine of information as to the literary and social conditions of the time, and are the most reliable authority for the history of humanism in the Carolingian age. . . .

The work that Alfred did for education was prodigious. Professor Pfister writes:

> . . . The Anglo-Saxons and the Italians brought to the Franks the treasures they had safely guarded; the Emperor Charles the Great recognised that it belonged to the duties of his office to spread enlightenment, to foster art and literature; and at length, after this night of darkness, there shone forth the brilliance of a true renaissance.

What that something other than collecting books must have been, to earn for them the title of humanist, is not related in any work by a scholar of the period. Indeed, it may be said that the fourteenth-century passion for classical authors was so great that they overlooked the fact that man—his aims and aspirations—was worthy of their practical attention. The so-called humanist movement, strangely enough, affected only the well-to-do who could afford to indulge the desire to discover and study ancient works of literature and art.

So far as this influenced the schools, religious and moral training was indispensable, and we are told that Lactantius was one of the favorites of the humanists and that they read Augustine, Jerome, and Cyprian. Pope Nicholas V was a humanist, and he employed scholars to translate the Greek prose writers. The works of the men of literature in the movement, such as the satires of Filelfo and Beccadelli's *Hermaphroditus* were somewhat salacious, if not obscene.

Notwithstanding the charge that has been made against the humanists of that period as opponents of the Christian religion, Dr. Tilley points out: "To the very close of the fifteenth century the Church and humanism were in close alliance."

However, it was the painters and sculptors who were the real humanists, for in their representations, they pictured man as they saw him. Their models were very often their personal friends, and anyone who has made a study of the masterpieces of that period cannot doubt that they were familiar with the virtues and the frailties of the persons they bequeathed to posterity on canvas and in marble.

It is curious that the writers who have given us so much information on the Italian Renaissance seem to have overlooked the importance of Richard de Bury. He had reached manhood before Petrarch and Boccaccio were born. Edward III made him Bishop of Durham, Treasurer of the Kingdom, and Lord Chancellor. He wrote a unique book called *Philobiblon*, and in it we find dissertations upon volumes of the classics, which no other work of the period contains. We may infer from this that England at that time possessed a library of ancient works superior to any known to the humanists in Italy. Henry Morley tells us:

> . . . He [Richard de Bury] loved books, and gathered them
> from all quarters into a Library which he valued, not as a
> collection of rarities to be wondered at, but as a company of
> friends and teachers to be used. Any real student who desired
> to consult books might knock at the door of his palace at
> Bishop's Auckland, and be lodged and boarded while he
> stayed to make his references.

Certainly such a man should be included in the list
of those humanists who were lovers of books.

Humanism has been defined as the cult of antiquity,
and those who have studied the revival of learning
which burst upon Europe at the beginning of the
fourteenth century reveal plainly enough in their essays
that only the few who were in a position to collect
ancient works enjoyed the pursuit. Certainly men in
general lived and worked in quite another sphere and
were mainly occupied with the sordid concerns of
making a living. The great collectors had little knowledge of the real life of the people and cared less about
their human aims and aspirations.

It may be held, as Dr. Tilley suggests, that the
movement was in the direction of an "emancipation
from the tutelage of the Church in the cities of northern
Italy." However, that may be no more than a coinci-
dence for before Petrarch and Boccaccio were born,
there were many instances of a revolt among the people
against the exactions of the monasteries and the nobles.
Be that as it may, the passion for classical literature
and culture took hold and spread rapidly as an avocation
among rulers, their writers and artists. Moreover, the
people engaged in this estimable work convinced themselves that they believed in "the goodness of human
life and in the dignity, even in the perfectability, of
man."

But when we look into the economic and political
history of Italy, France, and England, we often find
conditions during the fourteenth century that do not
reveal all that has been granted to the humanists. The

right of criticism and free inquiry, which was claimed by those who indulged in the cult of antiquity, was not extended to the producers of wealth. It was an individualism for the few. Moreover, the powerful ones were frequently at war and made things very uncomfortable for those who did not dare to exercise the right of criticism. Indeed, soon after Petrarch passed away, there were peasant uprisings in Europe and in England where the nobles were enclosing the free lands of the people by force.

After the Black Death, the humanists in England raised no outcry against the Statutes of Laborers. Nor have we any record of champions, followers of Petrarch and Boccaccio, appearing in France and Italy to voice the rather large claims made for man in general. Quite the contrary! Until the appearance of Colet and Erasmus the humanists gathered under the banners of the opposing factions and discovered that the utopia of their dreams was no nearer to them than it had been to the murdered Cicero and the neglected Confucius.

It was not until after the Wars of the Roses that another movement to which the name humanism has been attached appeared in England. Under the tutelage of William Grocyn, a Fellow of New College, Oxford, there gathered a company whose names meant more to men in general than all of those who were famous in the Italian Renaissance. That this movement in England differed profoundly from the one in which Petrarch and Boccaccio were engaged is plain because the leading figures were associated with the Church. Grocyn lectured at St. Paul's when John Colet was dean, and Erasmus found a friend in Archbishop Warham. Erasmus wrote:

> . . . I have given up my whole soul to Greek learning, and as soon as I get any money I shall buy Greek books—and then I shall buy some clothes. . . . I have found in Oxford so much polish and learning that now I hardly care about going to Italy at all, save for the sake of having been there. When I

listen to my friend Colet it seems like listening to Plato himself. Who does not wonder at the wide range of Grocyn's knowledge? What can be more searching, deep, and refined than the judgement of Linacre? When did Nature mould a temper more gentle, endearing, and happy than the temper of Thomas More?

This period, which began with Henry VII, would better bear the name of "rebirth" than the one started in Italy nearly two hundred years earlier. The desire for knowledge was noticeable not only in the universities that had become almost decadent, but in the Church itself. The King looked upon this quest for "the New Learning" with favor. And when Colet stormed from the pulpit of St. Paul's that the time had come for a complete reformation in the Church, beginning with the bishops, Henry defended him and told him to go on with his work. He said: "Let every man have his own doctor, and let every man favour his own, but this man is the doctor for me."

The spirit of the universities was revived, and one writing at the time says of the influx of new students: They "rush to Greek letters, they endure watching, fasting, toil, and hunger in the pursuit of them." However, when the King invaded France and was driven to conclude a peace, Colet declared from his pulpit that to see Henry turn into a vulgar conqueror was a bitter disappointment. And he cried, "An unjust peace is better than the justest war." Moreover, Erasmus departed from Cambridge shocked at the madness around him, which led him to declare:

. . . It is the people who build cities, while the madness of princes destroys them. Kings who are scarcely men are called "divine"; they are "invincible" though they fly from every battle-field; "serene" though they turn the world upside down in a storm of war; "illustrious" though they grovel in ignorance of all that is noble; "Catholic" though they follow anything rather than Christ. Of all birds the Eagle alone has seemed to wise men the type of royalty, a bird neither beautiful nor musical nor good for food, but murderous, greedy, hateful to all, the curse of all, and with its great powers of doing harm only surpassed by its desire to do it.

This marked the first revolt of a humanistic character by men of learning and influence in the interests of the people. It is amazing to read the story of how the cultural war initiated by these scholars was carried into the palace of the King and up to the very altars of the churches. Then Erasmus brought out his New Testament, and we learn "the Court, the Universities, every household to which the New Learning had penetrated, read and discussed it."

But the humanism that directly concerned the aims and aspirations of the endeavors of man appeared in More's *Utopia*, in which he charged the society round about him as "nothing but a conspiracy of the rich against the poor." He tells us:

> . . . The rich are ever striving to pare away something further from the daily wages of the poor by private fraud and even by public law, so that the wrong already existing (for it is a wrong that those from whom the State derives most benefit should receive least reward) is made yet greater by means of the law of the State. . . . The rich devise every means by which they may in the first place secure to themselves what they have amassed by wrong, and then take to their own use and profit at the lowest possible price the work and labour of the poor. And so soon as the rich decide on adopting these devices in the name of the public, then they become law.

It is in this unique work of Thomas More that we gather evidence of the grave change in economic conditions that affected the peasantry. He tells us of the enclosures made by force and how the people were driven from the land to make room for the sheep. Certainly a spirit of humanism was sadly wanting to relieve the impoverished people. Even then, progress in culture and learning seemed to go hand in hand with penury and want. But the humanists fared ill in any endeavor they made to set conditions right.

Next came Luther, who would have none of the New
Learning. Reason to him was an evil and, after the so-
called Reformation, the great revival which began under
Henry VII suffered severely under the religious antag-
onisms that arose and the agrarian discontent caused
by the enforced enclosure of the common fields and waste
lands. Latimer has left a clear account of the vast
changes that had taken place within his own lifetime.
Moreover, the cost of war had emptied the treasury,
and, as More points out, cut-throats, thieves and
vagabonds increased in number notwithstanding the
heavier penalties the new statutes imposed. He proclaimed, "If you do not remedy the evils which produce
thieves, the rigorous execution of justice in punishing
them will be vain." Perhaps this was the last time in
any humanist movement that such patent common sense
was spoken.

It is impossible in a short essay to cover the ground
adequately from the end of Elizabeth's reign until the
rumblings of the French Revolution were heard. Never
before in history were so many champions interested in
the betterment of men in general, as were the leaders in
France when the great reform movement of liberty,
equality, and fraternity began. From Robespierre to
Condorcet, from Danton to Marat, the ideals of humanism poured forth in copious phrases, while from the
guillotine in Paris heads tumbled into the basket, and
the other parts of France suffered a long period of
shocking disorder. Every man suspected his neighbor,
and treachery was the order of the day. Grand phrases,
depraved creatures! The aims and aspirations that were
to guide men to a better condition of affairs were lost
in a sea of blood.

When the great change took place which marked
the turn from the humanism of the Middle Ages, it is
difficult to say. At any rate, the cult of antiquity, as it
was known to Petrarch and Boccaccio, disappeared from
the scene before the rise of Puritanism, and only echoes

of it were heard from few in the halls of learning. Later, when rationalism became the vogue with certain thinkers, little thought was expended upon the aims and aspirations of man. Indeed, it may be said that the aesthetic and cultural pursuits of the well-to-do for the period when the English Whigs were in the ascendancy affected comparatively few collectors of works of art and rare books. It is hard to think of a well-known rationalist who showed the slightest inclination to follow the cult of the Italians of the early fourteenth century. What followed was in the nature of an almost complete departure from the pursuits of the medievalists both in society and in the Church.

The reverberations of the French Revolution had scarcely died away when there was born one whose writings were largely responsible for the creation of a new school of humanists, who assumed great influence in England and America during the last half of the nineteenth century. Auguste Comte formed the Positive Society, and to his altar of rationalism there flocked many to worship the new god that he had created—humanity. He it was who dreamed of a science of society, and the principles and laws devised by him for a new utopia not only affected politicians but philosophers. It seems unbelievable now that the church of Comte should have been seriously considered by the utilitarians in England and in France. For they were associated with what was regarded as the great advance in scientific thought and the knowledge that was evident everywhere that society in the lump had failed to come anywhere near the realization of other dreamers, who had devoted themselves to its reformation.

Perhaps Comte expected too much of man and never got close enough to him to understand his waywardness. Otherwise he would not have announced:

> . . . In the name of the Past and of the Future, the servants of Humanity—both its philosophical and its practical servants—come forward to claim as their due the general direction of

this world. Their object is to constitute at length a real
Providence in all departments,—moral, intellectual and
material. Consequently they exclude once for all from political supremacy all the different servants of God—Catholic,
Protestant or Deist—as being at once behindhand and a
cause of disturbance.

However, it was clear to many before the twentieth
century was ushered in that the servants of humanity
were expending their efforts in vain upon those they
sought to edify. The Providence of Comte failed to
direct the departments of the State. Never was the
world in such an intellectual riot as it was before
World War I blasted the claims of the humanists. Indeed,
some of them admitted long before the war was over
that society in general was better fitted for a madhouse
than for a "definite social State, in which all means of
human prosperity will receive their most complete
development and most direct application."

The truth of the matter was that man showed not
the slightest inclination to be reformed, according to
the notions of philosophers and politicians. He, who
knew where the shoe pinched, had a vague idea that
the ethics of the Positive Church did not touch the
cause of his daily woe. It did not strike Comte that
Confucius had a better notion of what was wrong when
he said: "If right principles ruled through the kingdom,
there would be no necessity for me to change its state."
It might be said that the medieval and classical authors
had a far deeper understanding of what was at the root
of man's troubles than Comte had.

The secret of its failure lay in the notion that the
Positive Philosophy was to be a victory of the social
feeling over self love, or altruism over egoism. It is true
that Comte saw the necessity for a moral tranformation
in society as the first step toward the goal. However,
it was a mistaken altruism that preceded the attempt at
a moral transformation. This brought about a philanthropy in politics and society which undermined the

idea of those rights of man which had animated the souls and minds of the Physiocrats, including Turgot and the English philosophical economists, from the time of Hooker and Locke down to Adam Smith, Thomas Paine, and Cobden.

It is not so strange as some students of these political and social creeds imagine that, when the Positive Society was founded, Marx and Engels wrote the *Communist Manifesto*. Moreover, Bakunin and Proudhon were busily engaged in formulating basic reforms for humanity which in idea differed fundamentally from that of Comte. As for the men and women who were to become members of the Positive Church and worship the great being Humanity, they showed their discontent with conditions by starting revolutions in different parts of Europe. And when they failed to set up governments after the pattern devised by their leaders, their political masters, almost scared out of their wits, started to pack the statute books full of ameliorative measures which were in the nature of sops and doles, as a means of keeping them quiet. The only two effective changes were wrought in England by the abolition of the Corn Laws and in Gladstone's budgets by the remission of taxes, which bore hardly upon the wages of labor.

Bureaucratic humanism ran riot, once the government lent itself to be a milch cow to pacify the discontented. All sorts of private and church societies sprang up to do something for the poor, and even as early as fifty years ago, those who went into the distressed districts of the large towns often heard the jibe thrown at the altruists, "What a pleasure it is to do something for the poor!" Even the comic papers presented pictures of amateur well-to-do parish visitors giving advice formulated in drawing rooms of how to nurse children of the wretched and provide them with proper nourishment.

When the humanists realized that the legislation enacted for the relief of poverty and its attendant ills

called for a larger bureaucracy, not a few admitted that
it was time to try some other way to better conditions.
But once parish relief and the dole were begun, it was
impossible to turn back, and the greater the bureaucracy
engaged in this work grew, the more need there was for
largesse to keep the distressed people quiet. The student
has only to turn to the record of the legislation that
reached the statute book during the eight years before
World War I to be convinced of this.

There were a few right-minded critics of the new
system who did not hesitate to point out that man was
perfectly capable of attending to his own affairs if he
would only take the trouble to know the causes of his
material afflictions. One hundred years ago he had a
definite idea of what his rights were; otherwise, the
great advances that were made here, in England, and on
the continent of Europe could not have been achieved.
Grudgingly, his political masters bowed to some of his
demands, and at one time it seemed to thinkers who
were not utopians that they saw the gleam of a new day.

Thoughtful working men during the political campaigns of forty years ago were saying to their parliamentary leaders, "Leave it to us. We know what we
want." This cry is not heard today, and so long as the
bureaucracy can purchase the votes by bribes and doles,
there is little chance of such a demand being made again.

False altruism and spurious philanthropy have been
largely the undoing of the masses. According to the
reports made by government bureaus of investigation,
man has been emasculated. The churches submit to the
notion that the Creator bungled the whole job by not
providing a source large enough to supply the desires
and needs of His creatures—a blasphemy that can
scarcely be matched. No wonder some are inclined to
the notion that the vast majority of humans may be
classified as men only because they walk upright.

For a thoroughgoing review of the position in which
we find ourselves today, there is nothing quite like the

Gifford Lectures of Dr. Macneile Dixon, *The Human Situation*. This critique is not only the most powerful one that has come from the pen of a philosopher of this generation; it is, besides, the most essential for a proper understanding of the course that we have taken. Here we have a wide learning combined with a shrewd knowledge of man and his potentialities. There is not an activity of spiritual and physical existence that is overlooked in this work. The author says: "Men ask for nothing from the universe save justice, and they have not obtained it."

Here the key word implies everything fundamentally, and by it Dr. Dixon means the justice that was in the mind of Socrates and Jesus. If men as individuals cannot take care of themselves, why should altruism and philanthropy be given to save them from the fate that they deserve? In *The Human Situation* we read:

> . . . In their anxiety for human welfare, in their collectivist schemes, the sentimentalists have overlooked the individual man. They submerge him in the sea of their universal benevolence. But who desires to live in the pauperdom of their charity? Every man desires to be his own architect, and the creator of his own design, the sentimentalist himself among the rest. And the last and greatest insult you can offer to the human race is to regard it as a herd of cattle to be driven to your selected pasture. You deprive the individual of his last rag of self-respect, the most precious of his possessions, himself. If you treat him as a thing, an inanimate object which can be pushed hither and thither, if you treat him as one of a drove of oxen, you take away his birthright, and for this loss nothing can compensate him, not all the soothing syrups and honeys of the world.

This is to the point, and the denunciation is not a bit too strong. And, yet, the humanists who flocked into the political arena after the turn of the century were sincere men and undoubtedly thought their efforts would relieve the wretched. When one thinks of these rationalists—many of them declared followers of Comte —it is hard to understand why they imagined their indiscriminate charity, their altruistic schemes would in any way alter the conditions that were responsible for the deepening poverty. No wonder Bishop Creighton lost patience with some of them and said they are "as good as gold and fit for heaven, but of no earthly use."

The dole is the paltriest substitute for justice. Indeed, it should now be patent to everyone that it has been a cruel deterrent, for had it not been for the false altruism that spread like miasma into the halls of legislatures, it might have been possible before World War I to deal with fundamental reform here and in England.

Such a book as *The Human Situation* is not only a spiritual tonic that should be taken by our sociologists; it is a revelation of the nonsensical beliefs and the legislative stupidities of this generation. The all-round knowledge of Dixon is in itself a magnet that draws the reader on and on in the most convincing manner. No one who has written in recent years upon the conditions of the world has a higher appreciation of man than he has. And his appeal to the churches, the scientists, and the politicians to let him express himself and face economic pressure according to the tradition of the race should be irresistible, if they mean business.

There is the choice that must be made at once. It cannot be put off much longer. It is the choice that was offered by Moses—life or death; the one presented to every civilization of which we have record. If it be life, then justice is the essential. If not, neither rationalist nor humanist can save man from the fate that he has earned.

IX

The Corn Law Rhymes

FROM TIME TO TIME, THE NATIONS OF EUROPE HAVE provided us with songs of poetic national ardor which linger in our memory. Three might be mentioned, which will be sufficient to set us thinking of others: *Rule Britannia*, *The Marseillaise*, and *Deutschland über Alles*. The songs of the Italians in Garibaldi's day were sung by children long after he left the scene. The Greeks, too, chanted their national hymns when Byron was at Missolonghi; and the Poles were rich in folk song, the themes of which are distinctly noted in Chopin's piano pieces. Most of these, however, were cries for political liberty, and perhaps that is the reason why some of them are remembered.

England of the days of James Thomson and Cowper indulged in national hymns of a strident character. *Rule Britannia* and *The British Grenadiers* can scarcely be surpassed in comic braggadocio. National aspirations can, of course, be carried to excess, and small wonder that, at different times, the French and the Germans have poked fun at the English for their extravagant claims.

Washington Irving, in *The Sketch Book*, had a good-humored tilt at John Bull's bellicose nature. Other Americans took far too seriously the claim of Thomson in *Rule Britannia*.

> When Britain first, at heaven's command,
> Arose from out the azure main. . . .
> This was the charter of her land
> And guardian angels sung the strain. . . .

125

In recent years the English poured scorn upon *Deutsch-land über Alles*. There is something amusing in all this, because so much of the sentiment depends upon who is your political and military friend at the moment. Still, we cannot overlook the fact that national songs have their value as rallying media when a crisis arises.

There are songs that are not national, which left their mark upon generations of folk—these were economic and social. Somehow they are little thought of today, but they inspired wonders, accomplished by the masses in making their grievances known to the powers that oppressed them.

About the middle of the thirteenth century, William Langland wrote his poem, *Piers Ploughman*. In this we find a vivid description of the condition of the common folk of his day. Concerning that period there has recently been published the story of *The Peasants' Revolt, 1381* by Philip Lindsay and Reg Groves. It is a remarkable historical document and should not be overlooked by students who are working upon the economic history of the English people, for the book contains much new matter, and places the revolt in its true setting.

Lines from Langland's poem inspired impoverished men and women for generations, and perhaps gave them courage to voice their grievances in many crises. The people who rallied to the standards of Wat Tyler and Jack Cade were illiterate peasants, but they learned from poor clerks in minor orders the significant passages to be found in such poems as *Piers Ploughman*.

There was nothing of nationalistic boastfulness in these odes. They revealed a plight of the people that was one of despair, and for centuries John Ball's question was asked:

> When Adam delved and Eve span
> Who was then a gentleman?

This was an echo of the lines to be found in *The Anglo-Saxon Chronicle:*

At the beginning we were all created equal; it is the tyranny of perverse men which has caused servitude to arise, in spite of God's love; if God had willed that there should be serfs, He would have said at the beginning of the world who should be serf and who should be lord.

A long history lies behind the revolts of the masses, centuries before the Corn Laws were abolished, but it is in this last period I would search for those songs that reached the ears of statesmen and forced them to redress the grievance of the wretched.

The names of the poets who wrote the verses the people learned and sang for a generation before the Hungry Forties include many of the highest rank. Burns, Wordsworth, Shelley, Byron, and many others are an array of men whose genius can scarcely be surpassed by those of any other land. Byron's clarion cry rang out:

> Snatch from the ashes of your sires
> The embers of their former fires;
> And he who in the strife expires
> Will add to theirs a name of fear
> That Tyranny shall quake to hear.

From one end of the land to the other, the poets gathered to express the woes of the people and to urge them to make their poverty known and demand justice. In Burns' lines there is the same strain that we found in *Piers Ploughman*.

> What tho' on homely fare we dine,
>   Wear hodden gray, and a' that;
> Gie fools their silks, and knaves their wine—
>   A man's a man for a' that.
>   For a' that, and a' that,
>   Their tinsel show, and a' that;
>   The honest man, though e'er sae poor,
>   Is king o' men for a' that.

"Man's inhumanity to man" was the theme of the peasant-poet of Scotland; and nobleman Byron—rich poet, poor poet, too—took up the strain, all in the long tradition since the days of William Langland.

What a history it is, and how little we regard it today! Perhaps we need another James Russell Lowell to remind us of our duty and also of the work to which Lincoln set his hand. We talk so glibly about freedom and liberty and "our way of life" that a stranger would think, to hear us cackle, there was no such thing as poverty and restriction in the land. Lowell wrote:

> Is true freedom but to break
> Fetters for our own dear sake,
> And with leathern hearts forget
> That we owe mankind a debt?
> No! true freedom is to share
> All the chains our brothers wear,
> And with heart and hand to be
> Earnest to make others free!

A daring Wordsworth, if there were one today, might write:

> The world is too much with us; late and soon,
> Getting and spending, we lay waste our powers:
> Little we see in Nature that is ours;
> We have given our hearts away, a sordid boon!

Long before the Corn Law rhymers set to work, the sound of distant thunder was heard in many poems. Goldsmith's *The Deserted Village* must have reminded many a vicar of a small community of the desolation caused by enclosure of land by force and by Act of Parliament. The exodus from the country to the towns created a congested labor market and drove wages down to the point of penury.

Perhaps it was George Crabbe who sounded the first alarm in his poem, *The Village*. There he describes the condition of the parish workhouse:

> Theirs is yon house that holds the parish poor,
> Whose walls of mud scarce bear the broken door;
> There, where the putrid vapours, flagging, play,
> And the dull wheel hums doleful through the day;

There children dwell who know no parents' care;
Parents who know no children's love dwell there;
Heart-broken matrons on their joyless bed,
Forsaken wives, and mothers never wed;
Dejected widows with unheeded tears,
And crippled age with more than childhood-fears;
The lame, the blind, and, far the happiest they!
The moping idiot and the madman gay.

This awful picture of "the place of refuge" of England's poor contained perhaps the spark that fired the imagination of many a poet that came after its author. Sir Walter Scott, in his last days, often asked for some poems of Crabbe to be read to him. And Cardinal Newman considered *Tales of the Hall* to be "one of the most touching in our language." Its author is now forgotten, but his place in the revolt against poverty is assured.

Byron has described in *The Age of Bronze* the condition of England and the ambition of her landlords. In this poem he presents to us the statecraft, the foreign policy, and the futility of her recurring wars as no one else has done:

Alas, the country! how shall tongue or pen
Bewail her now *un*country gentlemen?
See these inglorious Cincinnati swarm,
Farmers of war, dictators of the farm;
Their ploughshare was the sword in hireling hands,
Their fields manured by gore of other lands;
Safe in their barns, these Sabine tillers sent
Their brethren out to battle—why? for rent!
Year after year they voted cent. per cent.,
Blood, sweat, and tear-wrung millions—why? for rent!
They roar'd, they dined, they drank, they swore they meant
To die for England—why then live?—for rent!

Goldsmith had put this in a single line: "Laws grind the poor, and rich men rule the law." The poets were outspoken in that day and did not hesitate to speak fearlessly to those in authority about the woes of the hungry. The Merrie England of the maypole and the dance had been swept away as if a cyclone had struck the villages. Yet, there was merriment in high places, and there were revelry and mirth at court, and in the houses of the rich. It took long years to impress the government with the fact that the economic disabilities of the wretched should receive its attention. The influence and zeal of Lord Suffield were of no avail. Referring to the condition of the country, he tells us he could make no impression on Lord Melbourne, who looked upon the subject as a bore.

About that time Shelley wrote *Men of England*. The verses have the roll of thunder and are filled with the warning that the lightning will strike:

> Men of England, wherefore plough
> For the lords who lay ye low?
> Wherefore weave with toil and care
> The rich robes your tyrants wear?
>
> The seed ye sow, another reaps,
> The wealth ye find, another keeps;
> The robes ye weave, another wears;
> The arms ye forge, another bears.
>
> With plough and spade, and hoe and loom,
> Trace your graves, and fill your tomb;
> And weave your winding-sheet, till fair
> England be your sepulchre.

Perhaps the songs of Ernest Jones stirred the people more deeply than the poetic protests of Wordsworth, Byron and Shelley. Jones' *A Song of the Lower Classes* was remembered by country folk for two generations after it was composed. The writer of this essay has often heard an agricultural laborer whisper some of its pregnant lines, when no squire was about to hear him.

> We plough and sow—we're so very very low
> That we delve in the dirty clay.
> Till we bless the plain with the golden grain
> And the vale with the fragrant hay.

We're low, we're low—we're very, very low—
And yet when the trumpets ring
The thrust of a poor man's arm will go
Through the heart of the proudest king.

We're low, we're low—our place we know,
We're only the rank and file;
We're not too low to kill the foe,
But too low to touch the spoil.

If we had poets today who wrote such lines, I presume they would be condemned as outright proletarian propagandists inspired by Moscow. But when the deepening distress of the Hungry Forties could no longer be ignored by Parliament, no one had the temerity to castigate the poets who wrote memorable verse which revealed the shameful degradation of the folk. Moreover, there were by that time men in Parliament who knew the facts and presented them courageously to the government. Both Cobden and Bright, to say nothing of Villiers, called for redress of grievance; and so impressive were their demands that they converted Sir Robert Peel, whose government abolished the Corn Laws.

It is the fashion now, and has been since Marx's day, to question the sincerity of these free traders, accusing them of selfish aims and the desire for an abundance of low-paid labor. The people who are guilty of making this charge overlook the facts that not only Gladstone and Disraeli paid tribute to their honesty and courage, but that also the Conservative party, the landlords' one, after a few years became as free trade in sentiment as the Liberal party itself.

The statistics of the advance made in the industrial activities of the people after the abolition of the Corn Laws and after the breakfast-table duties were repealed by Gladstone, show the most astonishing recovery of individual welfare, without any assistance from the State, that can be found in the annals of any country.

The cry of the Corn Law rhymers was effective without the aid of a Wat Tyler or a Jack Cade. The poets

did more, perhaps, to convince the people that they
could save themselves than even Cobden and Bright succeeded in doing from the platforms. Wathen Call's *The
People's Petition*, written when the distress was most
painful in the Hungry Forties, was recited in full by an
old agricultural laborer at a political meeting as late as
1906:

> O Lords! O rulers of the nation!
> O softly clothed! O richly fed!
> O men of wealth and noble station!
> Give us our daily bread.
>
> For you we are content to toil,
> For you our blood like rain is shed;
> Then lords and rulers of the soil,
> Give us our daily bread.

The minor poets, who read the longings of the people
in their distress wrote what the miserable were thinking
and dared not mutter. Some of them described their
woe in the vernacular, and scores of lines that might
have been penned by a Shelley or a Byron can be taken
from their verses. Often they reach an elevation of
poetic quality that is surprising. In Gerald Massey's
poems there are many such lines. For example:

> And love should spring from buried hate,
> Like flowers from winter's tomb.

Tom Hood's *The Song of the Shirt* and Elizabeth
Browning's *The Cry of the Children* are so well known
that it is scarcely necessary to mention them. The poems
of Arthur Clough and Charles Mackey may be found in
the anthologies.

In *The Times Literary Supplement* of December 2, 1949,
there was a review of the work of Ebenezer Elliott. He
wrote *God Save the People*. It became known as "The
People's National Anthem," and it was sung at Non-
conformist religious services, and especially by the men
at the great Brotherhood meetings. Perhaps it was the

most popular of all the verse written by the Corn Law rhymesters.

It is hard to tell why the work of Ebenezer Elliott has been overlooked by some of the anthologists of a generation ago, for Carlyle's essay, "Corn Law Rhymes," written for *The Edinburgh Review* (1832), deals with one of the most extraordinary characters in England of that period. Elliott was a prosperous iron and steel merchant of Sheffield; indeed, one of the minor bourgeoisie.

The man who wrote *Dream of Enoch Wray* deserves to be remembered. Carlyle's essay is instructive for those who would understand the tribulations of the English poor in Elliott's day. He says in his review:

> . . . Alas, how many brave hearts, ground to pieces in that unequal battle, have already sunk; in every sinking heart, a Tragedy. . . . Must it grow worse and worse, till the last brave heart is broken in England; and this same "brave Peasantry" has become a kennel of wild-howling ravenous Paupers?

The writer of the review of Elliott's work, which appeared in *The Times Literary Supplement*, reminds us:

> . . . Between 1830 and 1840 he had risen to a position in English poetry in which his contemporaries looked on him as the peer of Crabbe and Burns. He counted his friends in all ranks of society. His sincerity and vigour had won him the respect of critics of widely differing views. He had been foremost in opening new fields for poetry and, in Herford's words, he may claim to have carried out that part of Wordsworth's poetic programme from which Wordsworth himself "averted his ken" and given his voice to

> > the fierce confederate storm
> > Of sorrow barricaded evermore
> > Within the walls of cities.

What the people would have done without the poets, for the generation that followed Waterloo, is hard to tell. Private members of Parliament might have succeeded at length in voicing their claims in the House of Commons and brought about relief. But such poems as were written were learned by heart by thousands who could not read, and were repeated at the firesides of those who felt the misery. The poem is remembered. The speech is forgotten. The latter serves for the time of the meeting, but the verse that described the condition of the mass touched the soul of those who had no chance to hear such men as Cobden and Bright.

The children of those who lived in the Hungry Forties remembered the lines, and for two generations after the abolition of the Corn Laws, old men who could tell the story of their parents' suffering would, if they had confidence in one, repeat the verse their illiterate fathers had learned.

Many of these poems were used by Socialists at their meetings fifty years ago, but apart from the desire for brotherhood, there is no socialistic sentiment in any of them. All that the people wished in the middle of the last century was to have a chance to better themselves by their own endeavor and enjoy the fruits of their labor. They desired relief from the crushing burdens imposed by the system of protection. This was the reason for the great battle that took place, and it was won in Parliament and not at the barricades.

Is it a poet that we need to make plain to our Congressmen that there are distresses now that afflict the people and should be relieved? Alas, our poets have other themes, and there seems to be no one, since Carl Sandburg wrote his early verse and Edwin Markham wrote his *Man with the Hoe*, to voice the thoughts of those who find our way of life no easy matter, with all the crushing taxation, the restrictions upon thought and speech, and the horror of war and its consequences.

Somehow we do not realize that a generation is poor indeed that has no poet to speak for the people. And the contrast between the versifiers today—their themes, their forms, and all the modern gadgets of style—is so wide, when compared with the men who championed the desires of the people over a hundred years ago, that old folk who remember vividly the history of stint and pain despair of finding a people's poet.

X

The Centenary of the "Communist Manifesto"

THE YEAR 1948 MARKED ONE HUNDRED YEARS SINCE Karl Marx and Frederick Engels were deputed to draw up a party program for the Communist League. They set to work upon this task at a time when Europe was experiencing one of her most serious political and industrial crises. The conditions in nearly every channel of activity in her principal States were shocking enough but, so far as the workers in industry were concerned, matters were near the breaking point. No two men ever grappled with a problem with more hope of success than Marx and Engels. The signs of victory for the cause they represented were in the air, and during the preceding year, when the Congress of the League had met in London, the signals of a triumph for the proletariat were many.

It is very difficult for the student of this generation to picture the deepening distresses of that day, and those who read the *Communist Manifesto* and cast it aside as a frothy document scarcely worth reading do so because their minds are fixed upon entirely different industrial and social conditions—so different, indeed, that those with which Marx and Engels had to deal seem absurd. Yet, if one desires to understand what actuated these men, it is necessary to turn to the history of Europe as it recounts the story from the time of the French Revolution until the failure of the upheaval of

1848. There are many excellent works that deal with this period.

It is sometimes claimed that the *Manifesto* was responsible for the insurrection in Paris of June, 1848. Others have imagined that its appeal brought forth the revolutionary uprisings that afflicted Germany and Austria. That it had a great effect, no one can deny, but the sore which ailed Europe had been festering for generations before Marx and Engels were born. However, the *Manifesto's* influence was short lived, and all the hopes that had been raised by the clashes in European States were frittered away within a twelvemonth, and conditions lapsed back again to something like their old cruel standard.

It is impossible to know what these conditions were and at the same time condemn the authors, as many did, for describing the turmoil of affairs which existed merely in their imaginative minds. One has only to read the great speeches of Cobden delivered in the House of Commons and in the country to find all the material he needs on the severity of the distress in England itself. Any reasonable person will be convinced that Marx and Engels did not exaggerate the gravity of the industrial crises.

England, however, was very little affected by the revolution of 1848. The Chartists made a demonstration in February and were determined to carry a petition to Westminster containing the famous six points, two of which were manhood suffrage and annual Parliaments. But this came to nothing, for special constables were called out and the petition was sent to the House of Commons in a cab.

Let us grant, then, that Marx and Engels had sufficient political and industrial reasons for calling a revolt. In every important State in Europe after Waterloo there were to be found men as earnest as Marx and Engels crying for reform; some of them, indeed, went much further and aided the revolutionary movements. A

writer in *The Times* (London), December 31, 1947,
reminds us that de Tocqueville, in the French Chamber,
in January, 1848, asked: "Can you at this very moment
count upon to-morrow? Have you the smallest idea of
what a year, a month, even a day may bring forth?"
The author of *Democracy in America* was no firebrand,
but his words are fraught with warning. He knew the
time had come when something must break or the people
sink lower in their distress. The penury of great masses
of the workers could no longer be endured, and those
who rose against the evils of the time imagined that
the overthrow of the governments in favor of a system
of Communism was the only change that could be
effective. This explains why the *Manifesto* began with
these sentences:

> A spectre is haunting Europe—the spectre of Communism.
> All the powers of old Europe have entered into a holy alliance
> to exorcise this spectre; Pope and Czar, Metternich and
> Guizot, French Radicals and German police-spies. . . .
>
> Communism is already acknowledged by all European
> Powers to be itself a Power.

It is not easy for the student of today to grasp the
significance of this astonishing declaration; therefore, it
is necessary to present a picture of what actually took
place in Europe at the time. I cannot describe, within
the compass of an article, the principal events of 1848
in a briefer way than has been done by *The Times* (London) writer in the article referred to above:

> . . . On January 2 Italian patriots, rising against Austrian
> misgovernment in Lombardy, had given the signal for the
> general uprush of liberal and nationalist sentiment which con-
> sumed Europe for more than a year.
>
> The heads of the most respected royal houses in Europe
> fled before the censures of popularly elected diets and students'
> unions. The King of Prussia was to be seen marching through
> the streets of Berlin with the German tricolor flying above
> his head, dutifully repeating the slogans of revolution to
> open-air meetings of undergraduates and working-men. Before

the year was out a free Press had been established in the
Papal States, and the Pope had appointed a lay administration. Metternich, the mainstay of the European order since
1815, joined Louis-Philippe as a refugee in England in the
spring.

Everywhere the revolution followed the same lines. Peti-
tions were succeeded by riots, riots by official capitulation,
official capitulation by the election of Constituent Assemblies
to define the Rights of Man and establish perfection. Sovereignty passed from landed aristocracies, field-marshals,
priests and secret police to poets, pamphleteers and scholars.
To liberals it seemed like the unconditional surrender of
power and privilege to intelligence; to conservatives like the
beginning of an anarchy which would not end until society
had been destroyed.

Let us now examine some of the salient points in the
Manifesto and try to understand why forty years later,
shortly after the death of Marx, Frederick Engels,
referring to the Paris Commune of 1848, said that it
had proved "that the working-class cannot simply lay
hold of the ready-made State machinery, and wield it
for its own purposes." This statement was incorporated
in the preface written by Marx and Engels in 1872 for
the German edition. There are many other reasons why
the revolution of that year, when the *Manifesto* was
issued, failed. The chief one was that Marx and Engels
were neither workers nor politicians, and they entirely
miscalculated the fitness of the proletariat for their
work at the barricades and also for conducting a system
of order that was essential for the inauguration of the
new era. They were right about the industrial conditions
that existed, but they were wrong about the means of
transference from the old order to the new.

Moreover, the terminology that they used had been
selected arbitrarily to serve the purpose of the propaganda of a class struggle. To show that this was so, it
is only necessary to take their two all-inclusive terms:
"bourgeoisie" and "proletariat" and quote their own
definitions of them. In a footnote we are told:

> By bourgeoisie is meant the class of modern Capitalists, owners of the means of social production and employers of wage-labor. By proletariat, the class of modern wage-laborers who, having no means of production of their own, are reduced to selling their labor-power in order to live.

The terms designating the two classes were so foreign to the minds of capitalists, risen from the ranks, and so strange to the ears of the laborers, in or out of work, that when they became current political gossip they suffered from many witty quips and not a few bawdy jokes.

It did not take long after the *Manifesto* was circulated, even among trade unionists of the time, for men in small businesses to ridicule the notion that they were oppressors even of the one or two apprentices they employed. And as for being a party of one class struggling against another, such a matter had never entered into their minds. Indeed, so far as Europe was concerned, the small business man had a far better understanding of economic law than the authors of the *Manifesto* had.

In England there was taking place a change so vital in the affairs of her people that it was not to be wondered why the appeal of the *Manifesto* fell flat. The Corn Laws had been abolished and were followed by successive budgets remitting duties that fell heavily upon the working classes. The purchasing power of the shilling rose, and long before Engels wrote his new preface to the *Manifesto*, the props had been knocked from under many of the ideas its authors held. The amazing leap forward that Great Britain made during the sixties and seventies (in spite of three severe trade depressions) indicated clearly to the working classes that taxation was a fine upon effort and that it was responsible for much of the penury of the artisans and the dislocation of trade and commerce.

But evil conditions were not abolished. The consequences of land monopoly were evident everywhere. Nevertheless, the improvement that was made was so patent to everybody that Tory and Liberal governments vied with each other in offering further and far greater reforms. Indeed, the change was so far-reaching that in 1867 the Tory party dished the Whigs and extended the franchise. Later, in the eighties, the agricultural laborer was admitted to the electorate.

The long, arduous fight for factory reform at length brought about beneficent changes. The formation of the co-operative societies of the workers was a development that had never been foreseen by Marx and Engels, and the success of these ventures would have been hard for them to explain. Whether the executives of the Wholesale Co-operative were to be classified as bourgeois capitalists and the shareholders who drew their dividends as proletarians, no one could say.

The story of the rise of the co-operative societies is a signal instance of what the so-called proletarians can do once they determine to better themselves. In 1916 Alice Stopford Green, in the Epilogue to her husband's great work, *A Short History of the English People*, gave a brief sketch of the success of this venture, which was not begun by bourgeois capitalists:

> . . . The Co-operative Wholesale Society, originated by a little group of artisans who met in Manchester over a "sixpenny tea," expanded during the next fifty years into a commercial enterprise exceeding any effort of private capitalism in its continuous success. Beginning with 24,000 members, it was in nine years serving 100,000 families; had started its own banking department which has now an annual turnover of nearly £20,000,000, and opened a boot factory with a present annual manufacture of nearly £8,000,000. It now manages five of the largest flour mills, and one of the largest tobacco factories; owns agricultural land in England and tea plantations in Ceylon: and is said to buy goods—and this for cash—at the rate of something like a thousand pounds in every minute of the working year. A scheme to protect the savings of the poor was inaugurated by Gladstone in the Post-Office Savings Banks, in which a fifth of the whole population now invest their economies: he also made it for the first time

possible for the working-classes to acquire small annuities without risk of fraud or bankruptcy.

This achievement could not have been realized if it had not been for the system of free trade which was ridiculed by Marx. Without a revolution, during the sixties and seventies, vast numbers of the British working people solved many of the problems that had distressed their forefathers. Of course everything had to be wrested from government, but the granting of the franchise in those days made the political powers recognize many of the important claims of the electorate, and all this was done by the so-called proletarians with no assistance from the Communists.

The *Manifesto* is sheer assertion from beginning to end—mere statement made by men who were far removed from the people they would liberate from the toils of the capitalist. The British working men had proved, by the time Engels wrote his new preface in 1888, that there was quite another way of solving economic and political problems than by raising barricades and overthrowing governments. It is amazing to think that the great experiment taking place under Engels' eyes did not indicate clearly to him that the *Manifesto* could be of no avail in Great Britain or in the United States. Yet, a century later Harold Laski asserted that "The *Communist Manifesto* still remains the most inspiring and up to date Socialist document."

The revolution of 1917 in Russia was the occasion for a revival of the doctrine in Central Europe. Since the time of Lenin's success, Communist societies have sprung up all over the world, and today there is not a State in Europe that is not seriously affected by the growth of the movement. Therefore, those who study the *Manifesto* at this time read into it entirely new matter with which it did not deal. Take, for example, the following:

> The Communists, therefore, are on the one hand, practically the most advanced and resolute section of the working class parties of every country, that section which pushes forward all others; on the other hand, theoretically, they have over the great mass of the proletariat the advantage of clearly understanding the line of march, the conditions, and the ultimate general results of the proletarian movement.

This claim was never substantiated, and the absurdity of it should have been patent to Engels. Indeed, within a year it was shown conclusively that the revolt had failed. There was not a single leader in "the line of march" who reached the enemy's trenches with the slightest chance of success.

In a way it is amusing to notice in the *Manifesto* the many instances of circumlocution, a consciousness, as it were, of uncertainty about the terms used and the intentions of its advocates. The following is an example:

> The distinguishing feature of Communism is not the abolition of property generally, but the abolition of bourgeois property. . . .

No Communist with whom I have debated the question has ever been able to state why two kinds of property should be differentiated. It may be that Marx and Engels realized, when they reached this part of their work, that there were possible adherents to the cause who were in small businesses and that it would have been detrimental to the movement to abolish the private property owned by these people. But they did not succeed in showing where the dividing line should be drawn. The great trouble was that they had no economic notion of what property is.

Assuredly it was difficult for them to prove that a man with a basket full of tools was *not* a capitalist and that a man with a factory full of tools *was* one! But they had no clear idea of what capital is. The nearest they could get to it was the industrial power of a factory owner to exploit the worker in an overstocked labor market.

The rest of the paragraph quoted above is as follows:

> . . . But modern bourgeois private property is the final and most complete expression of the system of producing and appropriating products, that is based on class antagonism, on the exploitation of the many by the few.
>
> In this sense, the theory of the Communists may be summed up in the single sentence: Abolition of private property.

So what they grant to the small man in the first part of the statement, they repudidate later on, unless, of course, there are *two* entirely different kinds of private property.

It was not until many years later (1867), when the first volume of *Das Kapital* was published, that Marx and Engels realized the true cause of an overstocked labor market, in which the unemployed competed against one another for jobs, and that this condition existed because the laborer had no alternative: he was a landless man. He had been driven from the soil.

There never was such an extraordinary economic rigmarole and such a confusion of ideas. "But does wage-labor *create any property for the laborer?* Not a bit. It creates capital, i.e., *that kind of property which exploits wage-labor.*" (italics mine) The authors did not realize that capital is *produced* and *not created.*

The sweeping denial in this quotation that wage-labor does not "create" (produce) any property for itself was disproved every day in the week, even at the time when the *Manifesto* was written. The Communist lecturer was often asked how working men could begin as small employers and afterwards enter the ranks of the "bourgeoisie" and become "capitalists," if they had no property. Surely most of the hated factory owners started from very small beginnings and were possessors of some property gained by their own exertions.

These were points raised in many debates in the early years of the controversy, before Fabianism and Socialism were discussed on political platforms. However, when the Labor movement in England veered in the direction of Socialism, the political platforms of England rang with challenge and opposition, particularly in the six years preceding the First World War. And it was during these campaigns that the hollowness of the *Communist Manifesto* was thoroughly exposed.

One of the principal passages from the *Manifesto* which suffered severely in debate is a curious example of the muddleheadedness of Marx and Engels:

> To be a capitalist, is to have not only a purely personal, but a social status in production. Capital is a collective product, and only by the united action of many members, nay, in the last resort, only by the united action of all members of society, can it be set in motion.
>
> Capital is therefore not a personal, it is a social power.
>
> When, therefore, capital is converted into common property, into the property of all members of society, personal property is not thereby transformed into social property. It is only the social character of the property that is changed. It loses its class-character.

I have known occasions when at question time the above has been read to Socialists with the demand that it should be explained in terms the audience could understand. And I never heard of any Socialist attempting to explain it. Why? Because the audience knew better than the speaker what capital is. Any plumber or carpenter in the audience knew that the tools he carried in his bag were capital and that he owned them. His social status was nil. Ask him if he regarded his capital as a social power; he would laugh.

But the greatest ridicule was poured upon the idea of the class character of capital. I remember a meeting in Yorkshire, in a spinning and weaving town where there was a large mill as well as several small individual and co-operative enterprises. At a meeting, the proprietor of the mill, a rich man, asked a Socialist lecturer to define his social status in production. This the lecturer failed to do, saying only that he employed labor. When the lecturer was asked into which class the employers in a small co-operative factory would fall, for a wonder he saw the absurdity of the position he had taken and laughed as heartily as anyone in the audience.

Further on we read about the proposals for the abolition of the family, and this is the way the case is presented:

> On what foundation is the present family, the bourgeois family, based? On capital, on private gain. In its completely developed form this family exists only among the bourgeoisie. But this state of things finds its complement in the practical absence of the family among the proletarians, and in public prostitution.

This was resented fiercely, and several of the men with whom I debated the question of Socialism versus Individualism told me that they did not agree with the statement and that it did an infinite amount of harm to the cause of Socialism. But the above-quoted sweeping denunciation is mild compared with the following:

> Our bourgeois, not content with having the wives and daughters of their proletarians at their disposal, not to speak of common prostitutes, take the greatest pleasure in seducing each others' wives.
>
> Bourgeois marriage is in reality a system of wives in common and thus, at the most, what the Communists might possibly be reproached with, is that they desire to introduce, in substitution for a hypocritically concealed, an openly legalized community of women. For the rest, it is self-evident, that the abolition of the present system of production must bring with it the abolition of the community of women springing from that system, i.e., of prostitution both public and private.

A comprehensive program was drawn up by the authors and, strangely enough, it contained several reforms advocated by the old Radicals. It is admitted in the *Manifesto* that the measures will be different in different countries, but "in the most advanced countries the following will be pretty generally applicable":

1. Abolition of property in land and application of all rents of land to public purposes.
2. A heavy progressive or graduated income tax.
3. Abolition of all right of inheritance.
4. Confiscation of property of all emigrants and rebels.
5. Centralization of credit in the hands of the State, by means of a national bank with State capital and an exclusive monopoly.
6. Centralization of the means of communication and transport in the hands of the State.
7. Extension of factories and instruments of production owned by the State; the bringing into cultivation of waste lands, and the improvement of the soil generally in accordance with a common plan.
8. Equal liability of all to labor. Establishment of industrial armies, especially for agriculture.
9. Combination of agriculture with manufacturing industries; gradual abolition of the distinction between town and country, by a more equable distribution of population over the country.
10. Free education for all children in public schools. Abolition of children's factory labor in its present form. Combination of education with industrial production, etc., etc.

This program was shelved for nearly seventy years, and when the time came to give it a trial, Lenin was in command and found difficulty enough in setting up a Socialist State. The experience of the past thirty years is that the Russian bureaucracy under Stalin has not brought about the "utopia" that Marx and Engels envisioned. But one thing is most noticeable in this experiment, which is that the proletariat still remains a proletariat. If it differs in any respect from the conditions prevalent in Europe at the time the *Manifesto* was issued, it is in the direction of solving the problem of an abundant labor market by forcible means, by a system of tyranny far more cruel than that which prevailed in the middle of the last century. What would Marx and Engels have thought of Siberian labor camps? It is true that the *Manifesto* calls for an *"industrial army,"* but no one would imagine that its authors dreamed for a moment of such a one as is under the command of the Soviet dictator today.

I do not know to what extent the *Manifesto* is read by Socialists at the present time. The clamor and the noise that are made about Communism are sufficient to impress one with the idea that the vast majority of people are busy studying the document and wondering when the next capitalist State will be overthrown. Day by day our newspapers devote columns to the question, but no one I meet seems to know what it is all about. None of my acquaintances indicates to me that he has read the *Manifesto*, and yet I hear Communism referred to week after week.

Perhaps the time has come when those who fear that this threat may become a political cataclysm should read this peculiar hodge-podge turned out by Marx and Engels and discuss its proposals and conceptions in the open.

In the preface written to the German edition of 1872 the authors stated: "The *Manifesto* has become a historical document which we have no longer any right to alter." Few people take the trouble to understand what was meant by this confession. The fact was that such extraordinary changes had taken place in the principal States of Europe that the *Manifesto* was antiquated and no longer effective as a program for the relief of the proletariat and the overthrow of capitalism.

XI

The Twilight of Marx

NINETEEN YEARS ELAPSED BETWEEN THE PUBLICATION
of the *Communist Manifesto* and the appearance of the
first edition of *Das Kapital*. What was Karl Marx doing
during this long interval? Undoubtedly he was collecting the material for his work. No one can read the
book without feeling that the painstaking industry
revealed in the copious footnotes was most unusual.
The author literally combed the sources at his disposal
and his work of research will stand as a tribute to his
perseverance. The fact that he was familiar with so
many languages and spoke four fluently was undoubtedly
a great aid in his quest for evidence.

When the critics pounced upon the work, some of
them remarked that Marx had chosen the sources that
suited his case and had ignored others that would have
refuted many of his conclusions. Few, however, chal-
lenged his findings as to the condition of labor in the
four leading countries of Europe.

The severest critic of *Das Kapital* was Eduard Bernstein who, in 1881, became the editor of the *Sozialdem-
okrat*. He was also associated with Karl Kautsky and
sat in the Reichstag before the First World War. It is
worth the while of any student of Marx's work to turn
to the article on him in *The Encyclopædia Britannica*,
which was written by Bernstein. There is to be found
an excellent summary of the objections made by the
Socialists themselves not only to the thesis of *Das*

Kapital but to the methods by which its author arrived at his conclusions. Bernstein says:

> Almost from the first *Das Kapital* and the publications of Marx and Engels connected with it have been subjected to all kinds of criticisms. The originality of its leading ideas has been disputed, the ideas themselves have been declared to be false or only partially true, and consequently leading to wrong conclusions; and it has been said of many of Marx's statements that they are incorrect, and that many of the statistics upon which he bases his deductions do not prove what he wants them to prove. . . .
>
> It must further be admitted that in several places the statistical evidence upon which Marx bases his deductions is insufficient or inconclusive. . . .

This is mild, however, in comparison with the thorough analysis of the whole Marxian theory presented by Bernstein in his *Evolutionary Socialism: a Criticism and Affirmation*. This work is scarcely known to the Socialists of today.

Still, it must be admitted that an industrial change had taken place before the German edition of *Das Kapital* was published. The work of reform, particularly in Great Britain, undermined some of the theories Marx formulated and nearly all the conclusions at which he had arrived. Therefore, it is necessary to consider the time lapse after he set to work to write his book. The improvement that took place in labor conditions between the time when the *Communist Manifesto* was issued in 1848 and the publication of *Das Kapital* in 1867 made all the difference between the prophecies laid down in the former and the declarations he reached in the latter.

Government statistics showed and the annals of Parliament revealed that while Marx was writing, the status of the working classes was gradually improving. Moreover, in some directions the proletarians were amassing capital of their own and starting businesses for themselves. This change that went on fairly steadily for the next two generations—in spite of three depressions—made the predictions ventured in the *Communist Manifesto* seem extravagant, if not absurd. Co-operative societies, building associations, penny banks, and numerous other institutions, fostered by the workers themselves, were springing up in every direction.

Parliamentary returns show that the income tax in Great Britain for the year 1854 was 1*s* 2*d* in the pound. Twenty years later it was 2*d* in the pound. In 1865 the national indebtedness amounted to over £800,000,000; thirty-five years later it had been reduced by £160,000,000.

Viscount Goschen, who was Chancellor of the Exchequer in 1886, delivered an address which, in his essays, is entitled "The Increase of Moderate Incomes." And to this he appends many of the statistics of government departments, which indicate the advance made in the condition of the working classes. It is an illuminating study to go through them, particularly if one keeps in mind the statements that were made in the *Communist Manifesto*. The increase in the number of working men's houses and of shops is given for periods in the last quarter of the nineteenth century. In ten years from 1875, the increase in dwelling houses of less than £20 ($100) rental a year nearly doubled. The number of building societies making reports in the ten years 1876-1886 increased from 489 to 2,079. The insurance companies of the poor made a return, showing that the annual premiums in five years were nearly doubled.

I could give many other instances of the gain that was made when taxation was reduced by Gladstone's budgets and the worker enjoyed a breakfast free of duties. Small wonder, then, that the British working man in those days did not accept the declarations and prophecies laid down in the *Communist Manifesto*.

After the Franco-German War, which lasted about ten months, something like a miracle took place in Great Britain, France and Germany, which made the predictions of a proletarian revolution overthrowing capital utterly unsound. From this it is not to be inferred that the working man had entered into a paradise and that he was secure from poverty. But he had shown by his own efforts, without the cataclysm imagined by the authors of the *Manifesto*, that he could, if he desired, make things better for himself.

This, perhaps, is the real reason why Marx was conscious, before he died in 1883, that the revolution he looked for was postponed until the Greek calends. Undoubtedly Engels, who put together the notes that formed the second and third volumes, knew before his death that the work had lost its significance, for in a letter, dated London, June 25, 1890, he deals principally with the trifling matter of whether a speech delivered by Gladstone was correctly reported by Marx. In this letter we find no such prophecies as those that were set down in the *Manifesto*.

Seventy-five years have passed since Marx wrote his preface to the second German edition of *Das Kapital*, in which he said:

> The contradictions inherent in the movement of capitalist society impress themselves upon the practical bourgeois most strikingly in the changes of the periodic cycle, through which modern industry runs, and whose crowning point is the universal crisis. That crisis is once again approaching, although as yet but in its preliminary stage; and by the universality of its theatre and the intensity of its action it will drum dialectics even into the heads of the mushroom-upstarts of the new holy Prusso-German empire.

There have been grave crises enough to satisfy the most belligerent revolutionary, but the proletarians have not brought them about. All these have been staged by the bourgeois politicians, to the utter discomfiture of millions of capitalists. The cost of the wars has done more to reduce the fortresses of capitalism in Europe than all the propaganda of the authors of the

Manifesto and *Das Kapital* has done. Marx and Engels never dreamed that politicians would serve their ends by disrupting the trade of Europe and Asia and placing on the workers burdens more terrible than their revolutionaries could have inflicted.

Alas, the workers, instead of overthrowing the enemy Marx and Engels invented for them, have found that it has been the other way about. They have been ground to powder by their governments.

Before the First World War, the Fabians of England had formed themselves into a polite debating society, which from time to time issued tracts, many of which might have been written by the Christian Socialists of that period. These tracts were undoubtedly critical but were read by only a small number of the intelligentsia. The Socialists, however, had entered the political arena. The first time one appeared as a candidate in a constituency was in 1906, when Victor Grayson won an election by a small margin in a three-cornered contest. This was not a very serious matter—not so serious indeed as the desertion of young men in certain trade unions from the Liberal cause.

The Social Democrats were so few that they made no impression at all, but served the purpose of organizing debates with opponents, and these were usually sparsely attended. Little was heard of the Communists, and many of the leaders in the several Socialist movements angrily repudiated the charge that there was scarcely any difference between Socialism and Communism.

Such was the situation, according to my recollection, from the period of the close of the Boer War until 1908. In France and in Germany there were strong political Socialist movements, and these had been in existence for many years—almost two generations. To what extent *Das Kapital* was studied by the members of these organizations, no one knew. And when I asked George von Vollmar, who sat in the Reichstag for a Bavarian constituency, about the education of the proletarians,

he told me that most of the information was imparted
to them from the platform or by leaflet. Such was the
case in France, and many of the Socialist leaders lamented
the fact that Marx's work was read so little. In England
I never came across a Socialist who knew anything
about it, and today when we hear so much about the
menace of Communism, I doubt that one in a million
has read the work.

Now why is this? The question should be put because
the terms "Marxist" and "Communist" appear in
articles in the public prints and seem to have a currency
much like that of the terms "Catholic" and "Protestant." Yet, I know only two living men who have
impressed me with the fact that they have studied *Das
Kapital*. Surely it is to be inferred that this book is
known now only by its title, and I think it is safe to
say that never was one talked about so much and read
so little.

State Socialists who shunned the political arena have
frequently remarked that since the theories of surplus
value and labor time were abandoned, the political
Socialists, who know of the repudiation, avoid the
theories with which Marx begins his book and now
concentrate upon Stalinism, which is a very different
order of things than Marx and Engels imagined could
exist.

Before Max Hirsch, in *Democracy versus Socialism*, submitted *Das Kapital* to carefully reasoned criticism,
Böhm-Bawerk in his profound exposition in *A Positive
Theory of Capital* had dealt a smashing blow at the
Marxian thesis. There were, moreover, many Socialists
who agreed with Hirsch that Marx's theory of value is
shown "to be a hypothesis ill-considered and unten-
able." Even the English Fabians repudiated it, and
Sidney Webb said:

> English socialists are by no means blind worshippers of
> Karl Marx. Whilst recognising his valuable services to eco-

nomic history, and as a stirrer of men's minds, a large number of English socialist economists reject his special contributions to pure economics. His theory of value meets with little support in English economic circles, where that of Jevons is becoming increasingly dominant.

It is a great pity that Max Hirsch's work is not found in every library of this country, and particularly in those of the universities. It is not a difficult book to read, and Hirsch's clear and penetrating style reveals the thought of Marx so simply that it can be studied easily. It was published in London and in New York by Macmillan and Company, in 1901. Some years ago I received permission from the publishers to issue a new edition of it, and perhaps the time is ripe for another one.

The changes, however, that have taken place concerning the value of Marx's work have been so considerable since the Russian revolution that it is a wonder to me someone has not gathered the main threads of the great controversies which arose about *Das Kapital*, and recorded them in an explanatory volume that would be of great use to students. If there be a dread of the Communist menace, it seems to me the best way to meet it is to inform the people, if they wish to be informed. The Socialists themselves in recent years have produced works that reveal the great differences of opinion which rage among them, and surely it must be reckoned as a very strange matter that few of the leaders in this country agree as to what Socialism is and what Communism is. Most of them admit that Stalinism differs entirely from the old doctrines.

In 1934 a work was published by the *American League for Democratic Socialism* which was called *Socialism, Fascism, Communism*. The foreword of the editors gives one an idea of the fog that exists in anti-capitalist circles:

> The purpose of this book is to present a point of view on burning questions of international Socialism and labor which has not had adequate representation in America. It is the

point of view of Social Democracy as distinct from the Communist, quasi-Communist and "liberal" points of view from which these questions are discussed in radical circles in this country. Even in circles more inclined to the Social Democratic approach to these problems, there has been a great deal of uncritical thought and confusion due largely to lack of information and to misinformation which have beclouded social thought.

Then in the introduction by Abraham Cahan we learn:

> . . . The abolition of private property in the means of production and transportation is the great goal of Socialists and Communists alike. When it comes, however, to ways of reaching it they are separated by a chasm as wide and deep as the one yawning between Wage-Slavery and the Co-operative Commonwealth. To Socialists a democracy which ensures representative government, personal liberty, free speech and an untrammeled press, is as essential as the economic part of their program. The one, in fact, is a necessary condition in the struggle for the other.

No Socialist of my acquaintance before World War I would have agreed that representative government was a necessary condition under which the abolition of private property could be brought about. Perhaps it would be better for Socialists to agree upon a precise definition of the term "property" and relegate all the absurd notions of Marx and Engels to the dust bin of fallacious theories.

Abraham Cahan is very sure that Communism is not Socialism, for he says:

> Dictatorship, on the other hand, is inevitably coupled with savage despotism and ruthless terrorism. It is a "hold up" on a country, with its people paralyzed by fear and tortured by the unspeakable outrages of concentration camps.

The above is an indication of how far Socialists and Communists have departed from the ideas held by the authors of the *Manifesto* and *Das Kapital*. But we see this cleavage and departure everywhere, and it is the greatest mistake to think that Communism is practiced in Russia. The proletariat does not rule there, and as for justice and freedom for all men and women, these ends are as far to seek under the Soviet dictator as the origin of life itself.

A man who has been in the thick of it wrote an article for a recent edition of *The New York Times Magazine.* It is called "A Vital Fact in the Battle of Ideologies." The author, Francis Williams, at one time edited the *London Daily Herald,* and until recently he was public relations adviser to Clement Attlee. Here is what he has to say about the difference between Socialism and Communism:

> British Socialism has a special and individual character because it has grown and developed from peculiarly British roots and has been influenced hardly at all by the Marxist philosophy. Unlike British Socialism, Continental Socialism springs from the same roots as Communism although it has sharply diverged from it theoretically and practically during it development. This divergence, which has steadily increased with the years, is due partly to the shape taken by the Communist ideology under the influence of Lenin and Stalin and partly to the effect of historical differences in the political development of western and eastern Europe.
>
> Both had their roots in the dialectical materialism of Marx and Engels. . . .

There is one article in the book, *Socialism, Fascism, Communism,* which deserves deep study, for it is a forthright critique of the position in which the protagonists of both these "isms" find themselves today. However, it was penned before the beginning of World War II. This review of the situation was written by S. Portugeis, who is described as a "distinguished Socialist journalist and publicist residing in Paris." He has provided us with as sound a review of the present condition as I have seen. He says: "The position of Socialism thus becomes tragic: the line of struggle for the least of inevitable ills becomes fatally the line of the greatest available compromise."

Further on he tells us:

> . . . An examination of the purely economic side of modern capitalist society will reveal a picture of gigantic growth exceeding even the boldest predictions of its apologists. What appeared to be mad phantasies decades ago are now historical anachronisms. During this period the capitalist system has been shaken by a great many economic crises, each of which led its opponents to believe in the advance of an imminent twilight of its hegemony. Yet each time capitalism rose again with new force, like Phoenix from its ashes.

Here Mr. Portugeis has in mind the depression which followed the crash in 1929. What he would write now after a review of the present situation in Europe would be deeply interesting. Certainly he would not fail to recognize that the opposing forces in the war had abolished private property in a form no Socialist or Communist would have thought possible. But the amazing thing about it all is that the people who ordered the destruction are sitting on the necks of the proletarians that have survived and are hindering them in every possible way from restoring the necessary capital for providing the means of subsistence. Capitalism in Europe now will take a long time to rise Phoenix-like from its ashes.

These terms that are bandied about so lightly— "Democracy," "Socialism," "Communism," and "Fascism"—must have definite meanings. Each one must stand for a single purpose. But what do we find? There is scarcely any agreement among the parties as to what they mean. Yet, if one desires to be clear about the terms, it is only necessary to go back to the controversies that were waged upon these issues fifty years ago. Men at that time examined them thoroughly and submitted them to philosophical questioning and analysis. With the help of the thoroughgoing State Socialists, their individualistic opponents, the British Radicals, were able to agree upon the following proposals and conceptions:

(1) The State shall control all the means of production, distribution and exchange

(2) *for the equal benefit of all;*

(3) the State shall have power over persons, their faculties and their possessions.

This formula was submitted to the severest critical examination, and it was found to be a logical statement of the aims of Socialism and Communism. But those who were afraid of State Capitalism would have none of it. Truth to tell, they saw in the distributive proposal *"for the equal benefit of all"* an utterly impossible provision. Moreover, the Socialists and Communists in Great Britain and other European countries took fright at the necessary third proposal because they realized that it meant the loss of liberty. No one knew quite what was meant by the term "liberty" but somehow they had an idea that the little they enjoyed was worth keeping.

Today there is not much left of the work of Marx and Engels but what is called "dialectical materialism." That all history reveals a struggle for economic salvation on the part of the masses against capitalistic institutions is only another way of putting the age-old problem of the fight for economic freedom. Neither Marx nor Engels was the first to deal with this matter. It can be read in the myths and histories of Egypt, the Hebrews, the Greeks, and the Romans. It differed only in degree when it was treated by the author of *Das Kapital*.

And now I wish to touch upon one of the strangest things that is to be found in the literature of this struggle, and that concerns the reason for the subjugation of the peasantry in every State of which we have record and the crowding into the towns of landless men to compete with one another for few jobs.

When Marx and Engels became conscious of this phenomenon it is difficult to say. But no one that I have read has explained why Marx put the cart before the horse in the first seven parts of his work. Not until the

chapter on "The So-called Primitive Accumulation"
does he give the reader the full story of the expropriation
of the tillers of the soil and, consequently, the conges-
tion of labor in the towns. How different his work would
have been if he had dealt with the cause of the evil
conditions before he touched the effect. It seemed as if
he was suddenly struck—after writing more than 700
pages—by the fallacy of his own creation, for he says:

> In the history of primitive accumulation, all revolutions
> are epoch-making that act as levers for the capitalist class
> in course of formation; but, above all those moments when
> great masses of men are suddenly and forcibly torn from
> their means of subsistence, and hurled as free and "unat-
> tached" proletarians on the labour market. The expropriation
> of the agricultural producer, of the peasant, from the soil, is
> the basis of the whole process. The history of the expropria-
> tion, in different countries, assumes different aspects, and runs
> through its various phases in different orders of succession,
> and at different periods. In England alone, which we take
> as our example, has it the classic form.

He then proceeds to recount, as an English Radical
would, the consequences of this conspiracy of the landlords. Overlook the false application of economic terms
and the indiscriminate way in which he uses them, and
little exception can be taken to the historical review
that he presents. As an instance of the confusion from
which he suffered, the following may be quoted:

> The spoliation of the church's property, the fraudulent
> alienation of the State domains, the robbery of the common
> lands, the usurpation of feudal and clan property, and its
> transformation into modern private property under circum-
> stances of reckless terrorism, were just so many idyllic
> methods of primitive accumulation. They conquered the field
> for capitalistic agriculture, made the soil part and parcel of
> capital, and created for the town industries the necessary
> supply of a "free" and outlawed proletariat.

It was not so much the church's property the spolia-
tors desired; it was their land, which is not property;

and they did not make the soil part and parcel of capital. Soil is created, and capital is produced. It is strange that Marx never saw this distinction which is so important to those who wish to understand the conditions which arose out of the theft of the source of man's subsistence.

But it is in the chapter on "The Modern Theory of Colonisation" that he fully realized that "the expropriation of the mass of the people from the soil forms the basis of the capitalist mode of production." And, yet, when he grasped this patent fact, he had no suggestion to make of a method by which landless men could once again have an alternative to entering an overstocked labor market. A proletarian revolution for the abolition of private capital was no way out of the difficulty. The revolution had failed in 1848-49, and it was found when the proletarians were defeated that private property had suffered little.

Socialists and Communists at the beginning of the century laughed to scorn the Radical notion that the matter could be solved by making labor scarce. The suggestion that the first necessary step in this direction was to take the rent of land and exempt the production of wealth from taxation seemed to them to reduce the whole matter to an absurdity. Some said such a simple proceeding was scarcely worth consideration; others said if you made men scarce in the labor market there would be no revolution. Some leaders of labor organizations said if workers were scarce there would be no need for trade unions. The truth of the matter is that none of the followers of Marx and Engels with whom I came in contact realized the wage question was the land question and that Marx himself must have seen this economic fact when he wrote his chapter on "The Modern Theory of Colonisation."

There is one other curious matter that has never been cleared up, and that is the reference to Haxthausen in the *Communist Manifesto*. It appears in a footnote, and

Engels admits in his preface, dated 1888, that he was responsible for adding "a few notes explanatory of historical allusions." Now this one on Haxthausen goes rather deep, for it refers to the "common ownership of land in Russia" and states that Maurer

> proved it to be the social foundation from which all Teutonic races started in history, and by and by village communities were found to be, or to have been, the primitive form of society everywhere from India to Ireland.

Surely it is amazing that our authors did not see the significance of the historical evidence they turned up about primitive communities and man's association with the land down to the period when enclosure was made by parliamentary statute at the beginning of the nineteenth century. It seems to me they learned the cause of the trouble too late and they had not the wit or courage to reconstruct the work upon a sound economic basis.

Shortly before Kautsky died, he lamented that *Das Kapital* was read by so few, and yet he knew that the basic ideas of surplus value and labor time had long been abandoned. There is no public today for Marx's work, not even the shreds that are left of dialectical materialism. All this has been done far better, because the recorders of our time who have dealt with the subject have applied themselves solely to it and have not been hampered by such a notion as abolishing private property and awaiting a universal proletarian revolution.

XII

State Control

A Backward Glance

I PRESUME IT IS THE BUSINESS OF PROFESSORS OF LAW AND sociology to explore the fields of economic and political activity and watch the revolutionary trends and movements that concern the mass of the people. Yet, it is seldom one comes across a book that appeals to a wide circle of readers, which in its unbiased treatment of such subjects bears the hallmark of a detached mind.

I have been asked many times in recent years to recommend a work that would reveal the changes in political thought so plainly that the ordinary college student would be able to understand it. I know of no such volume. Nevertheless, it would not be difficult for any intelligent person who had lived through the economic and political upheavals since the turn of the century to compile a record of the strange happenings that have brought about wars, Constitutional changes, and economic disasters.

One of the reasons why there is no desire on the part of the people to demand such an inquiry is that most of the politicians and nearly all the newspapers have directed the mind of the electorate to particular individuals and their personal associations with what are called un-American activities and not upon the movements that have carried them like straws upon a swift-running stream.

163

In a time of trade depression and increasing unemployment, what is more natural than the thought of impoverished men that there is something basically wrong with the economic system? For them, no statistician is needed to provide columns of comparative figures showing that wealth is unequally distributed. An empty belly is a convincing fact, and a hopeless morrow in the labor market is a prospect which saddens the mind. In this dilemma men seek a solution of their economic problems and are ready to grasp at any political or social nostrum that promises a change for the better.

It is not to be expected that men in such dire straits will question, much less doubt, the efficacy of the remedy they are urged to try. Experience of their grandsires goes for naught. Modern education has given them no information about past industrial crises that would enable them to judge the practical value of the "cures" for their woes.

They know nothing of the mass of literature which deals with the similar industrial conditions after the Napoleonic wars, and the intellectual battles that raged during the lifetime of Proudhon, Bakunin, and Marx.

Such subjects as Individualism, Anarchism, Socialism, and Fabianism have been dealt with in hundreds of volumes since Proudhon wrote *L'utilité de la célébration du dimanche*, which was the precursor of the revolutionary schools of thought.

Therefore, there is no reason for anyone to think that the masses who lend their ears to our propagandists know much about the "good tidings" of share-the-wealth schemes. The astonishing fact concerning the matter is that university alumni should advocate nostrums that were shattered in debate before they were born. Had they taken the trouble to read the story of the controversies of the propagandist intellectuals of the nineteenth century, the probability is they would have realized that discretion was the better part of revolution. For criteria there were at least twenty upheavals in European States after Napoleon was defeated, which might have served as restraints upon their ardor to plan utopias for wayward men. The books written by the American Fabians during that period revealed superficial notions of what they were advocating and little knowledge of the attempts that had been made to bring the workers into water-tight utopias by setting up governments of theorists and blueprint political architects.

The false reports that came from Russia, after the Treaty of Versailles was signed, led many of our writers astray. These were circulated by partisans, who believed Lenin was a Messiah who would, in time, solve the age-long problem of the unequal distribution of wealth and abolish involuntary poverty. When Lincoln Steffens came to see me, after his visit to Russia and his famous interview with the leader of the revolution, he told me there were many obstacles to be surmounted but that the future, although it had lengthened away considerably, was bright. Steffens, at that time, was no Socialist, but he was ready to ponder seriously any ideas for social betterment, and he accepted the Russian experiment as a necessary test of revolutionary methods to solve economic and political problems of long standing.

There were scores of other men here in the United States who thought as he did, and in the years from 1920 onwards, I did not meet one whose sincerity for drastic reform could be questioned. The only trouble I found about their notions was that none had given much thought to the history of the experiments of the nineteenth century, and that their faith in the masses for intelligent action, in their own interest, was not justified.

The men and women I met, during the life of *The Freeman* (1920-24), who thought at all of Communism, held only superficial notions of its proposals and con-

ceptions. Few had read the *Communist Manifesto*, and
fewer still had read the first volume of *Das Kapital*.
Strangely, nearly all these people called themselves
Liberals. They were, however, merely half-fledged
Fabians, but they did not know it.

Now in no case that has been tried before a judge and
jury, or one investigated by a Congressional committee,
has the question been raised as to the definition of such
terms as Communism and Socialism. Yet, in many
instances, the accused have been called Communists
and, strange to say, not one so charged, that I know
of, has asked for the term to be clearly defined. It would
be difficult, indeed, for anyone, in court or out of it, to
attach any other sense to the word than that it means a
revolutionary movement to overthrow the government.

Sixty years ago, hot gospellers were free to discuss
such subjects in the open. At that time I attended many
meetings in New York and Boston at which the speakers
denounced the government as a capitalistic institution
and advocated a change that would bring about a more
equal distribution of the wealth. I have heard Johann
Most, Tom Mann, and many other Socialist orators
preach from the *Communist Manifesto* and, in the last
words of that instrument, call upon the workers to cast
off their chains. No one was very much disturbed then
by these proceedings, and it would have been considered
absurd if anyone suggested that there were men in the
departments of the government who were secretly
attempting to overturn it.

There were Communists then who were theorists, but
there are no Communists now. For if there is one thing
Soviet Russia is *not*, it is that it is not a Communist
State. This statement may seem strange to the people of
this generation because Congressional investigations and
newspaper men have dinned into the public mind an
utterly false notion of what Communism is, as expressed
by *bona fide* State Socialists who took the trouble to
formulate a definition that would bear analysis.

Over fifty years ago, when Max Hirsch was collecting his material for his unique work, *Democracy versus Socialism*, he went carefully to work to find a definition that would be accepted by theoretical Socialists. And it was then formulated as follows:

> The State shall control all the means of production, distribution, and exchange for the equal benefit of all; and the State shall have power over persons, their faculties and possessions.

It should only be necessary to point out that such a State could not possibly be established. A utopia, in which wealth would be distributed for the equal benefit of all, is not for men, because they are men, no matter under whose rule they exist; moreover, there is no possible way of distributing wealth to men in equal shares. Those who advocated such a system were honest, sincere thinkers, who put it forward as an alternative to the system of an unequal distribution of wealth. It ought not to be necessary to point out that the Socialists themselves have always been the bitterest critics of those who enter the political field, who would try to bring it about increment by increment, and temporize with the catalytic principle.

The student has only to read the works of Philosophical Anarchists and Socialists at the time when Marx published his paper, to realize that the bitterest controversies raged among them for many years as to what gospel should be advocated and the means by which it could be established.

The Russia of today is as far from being a Communist State as anyone can imagine. There, the wealth is not divided for the equal benefit of all, although the government controls production, distribution, and exchange. It is a system of State servitude. Every person is at the beck and call of the government, and the severest penalties are imposed upon any infraction of its stern laws. The only understandable term for it is complete bureaucratic control. It is red tape, so tough and strong that it can be used as a noose to hang any recalcitrant who objects.

During the days of *The Freeman*, I came in touch with many young men who were dissatisfied with the condition of affairs and who looked for a change for the better, but I did not meet one who had any more knowledge of the difficulties that Lenin had to face than the veriest boy in the Student Movement. The taint of socialistic thought was evident in so much of their work that I advised one and all to study the books of Socialists and learn from them the many different interpretations of the creed. The information they had came from leaflets, pamphlets, and such papers as *The Masses* and other organs that promulgated notions of Fabianism.

About that time, I was invited to a reception at Harvard, given to honor Harold Laski. The reason why I accepted was a desire to meet the translator of Leon Duguit's book, *Law and the Modern State* (New York, B. W. Huebsch, 1919). Laski and his wife were responsible for the translation, but the introduction came from his pen. This work impressed me so deeply by its trend of thought toward revolutionary change that I decided to keep an eye on Mr. Laski and watch for the development of his notions. In his introduction to Duguit's work it is insinuated that the time had come when a change might be made in some of the provisions of our Constitution.

He says: "The very limitation of the much-criticized Fourteenth Amendment only means, as Mr. Justice Holmes has repeatedly emphasized, that legislation must be reasonably conceived, and adopt reasonable means of execution; and since that term is a matter of positive evidence, it is not a gate but a road."

This was the first warning I had of what was afoot. Further on in the introduction, Laski says:

. . . The decline of Congress, for instance, like the similar decline of Parliament and the French chamber, is to be interpreted in the light of its inability to cope with the new demands. *We have ceased to look upon historic antiquity as the justification of existence; it is the end of each institution of which we make consistent dissection and enquiry.* (italics mine)

These are passages the ordinary student of jurisprudence might regard lightly because he would not have a deep background of knowledge. To me they were significant pointers, marking a direction that might end in disaster. It is all very well and good, I presume, for theorists to speculate upon expedient changes in a Constitution—those a crisis would call for, but only necessary as ameliorative measures for the duration of the crisis. However, it is quite a different matter to strike at the fundamentals of such Constitutions as those of England and the United States and transmogrify them completely.

It was not until some years later that I learned about the spade work done by Laski during his visit to Harvard. When the Brain Trust made its appearance in the early thirties, the Harvard disciples of Laski soon revealed the ideas implanted in them by their teacher.

Early in the spring of 1933, there was a great outpouring of works upon the present system of the distribution of wealth and the restrictive canon of the Fourteenth Amendment, which says:

> No State shall make or enforce any law which shall abridge the privileges or immunities of citizens of the United States; nor shall any State deprive any person of life, liberty or property without due process of law, nor deny to any person within its jurisdiction the equal protection of the laws.

We had writings by Stuart Chase, Felix Frankfurter, Norman Thomas, Justice Louis Brandeis, George Soule, Justice Benjamin Cardozo, Rexford G. Tugwell, Mordecai Ezekiel, and many others. All of these particular works were devoted to what the authors considered to be necessary changes in our system.

In my book, *Sociocratic Escapades*, published in 1934, I was so conscious of the trend toward Fabianism in many of the New Deal supporters that I wrote:

> The task which some of the members of the Supreme Court seem to have set themselves is not only hazardous but one which will meet with increasing difficulty for many years to come. It is something quite new for jurists in a constitutional body to form themselves into a commission for investigating social problems; not only investigating these problems, but deciding the courses which should be pursued in remedying the defects of the economic system. It is a novel position for jurists to take up, and one cannot help wondering if those who suggest this change have deeply considered the extraordinary consequences of such an enterprise. Well might students ask if it be the intention of the Supreme Court to usurp the functions of legislative bodies.

The part played by Mr. Justice Holmes in this coterie organized by Laski, is quite clearly expressed in some of his opinions. Why he was set on a pedestal as a great jurist, I have never been able to understand, for many times he was swayed by economic and political affairs, remote from the functions of the jurist. These were concerns of Congress, not the High Court. In his decision in *Truax v. Corrigan*, he wrote:

> . . . The denial of the more adequate equitable remedy for private wrongs is in essence an exercise of the police power, by which, in the interest of the public and in order to preserve the liberty and the property of the great majority of the citizens of a State, rights of property and the liberty of the individual must be remolded, from time to time, to meet the changing needs of society.

I do not think it would be possible to find an example of such a declaration in English law. Whatever inequalities Holmes had in mind were matters that concerned the political body. The laws then on the statute books of the United States, if they had been enforced, would have been sufficient to remedy the defects. It would not have been necessary for Holmes, in a judgment from the bench, to ask for the Constitution to be "remolded from time to time." Somehow, Holmes never quite knew the difference between right and privilege, which was the crux of the problem.

Very similar ideas were voiced by other lawyers who were labeled "New Dealers." Justice Brandeis frequently expressed himself in terms not unlike those used by Laski. And, yet, on one occasion he said, "When a Court decides a case upon grounds of popular policy, the judges become, in effect, legislators." Indeed, it was part of the New Deal plan to put legislators on the Supreme Court bench.

When my books *Control from the Top* (1933) and *Sociocratic Escapades* (1934) were published, readers informed me they should have the widest circulation. I thought so, too, but the response of the reading public was not felt by booksellers, and only a small clientele showed any interest in them at all. Reviewers scorned to waste ink upon them. They died of neglect.

Still, some old-fashioned lawyers urged me to publish separately, in pamphlet form, the last chapter of *Sociocratic Escapades*, which dealt with the attack of the Laski-Holmes group upon the Fourteenth Amendment. They suggested an introduction to it written by a well-known jurist. Some were canvassed by my friends, but these were so busy they could not find time to write it, although they were convinced it should be done by someone. Nothing further was made of the suggestion, and the matter was dropped.

Then I was asked to write upon economic and political fundamentals. The president of one of our universities thought students should have a kind of primer in which they would find definitions of economic terms, and references to Constitutional law, ancient and modern, as it was interpreted by famous jurists. In *Man at the Crossroads* (1938) I made an attempt to supply my academic friend with the book he was looking for. It was widely reviewed but there was no great demand for it.

It was difficult for these small efforts, made for the purpose of enlightening the Philistines, to make much impression on readers, because a disastrous trade depression had fallen upon the country, and when the books were published, a Brain Trust went to work to plan a utopia that was to be promoted and fostered by a brand new President whose early orations betrayed the influence of notions sedulously sown by American and British Fabians.

"Soak the rich" was one of the slogans which caught the imagination of the empty purse carriers. Another one was taken from a book, called *A New Deal*, published in 1932, which asked: "Why should Russians have all the fun of remaking a world?"

Books, reviews, speeches, and debates revealed an extraordinary yearning for an administration of Fabians, supported by a Supreme Court of meek and lowly Municipal Socialists. In the *Yale Review*, Spring 1933, Felix Frankfurter said:

> . . . The capacity of States to control or mitigate unemployment, to assure a living wage for the workers, to clear slums and provide decent housing, to make city planning effective, to distribute fairly the burdens of taxation—these and like functions of modern government hinge on the Supreme Court's reading of the due process clause.

The outburst of the pent-up longings of the pupils of Laski brought forth works on how to put us all into an economic paradise, which amazed the wobbly British Liberals who had infiltrated the ranks of the Labor party. Such well-known writers as Walter Lippmann, George Soule, Adolph Berle, and R. G. Tugwell gave us the gospel of bureaucracy which was preached by professors, parsons, and politicians during the years 1933-39.

Some of the declarations of the planners of utopia have a strange tendency now to make us wonder if there could have been a time when they were held by the writers. Even as late as May, 1943, Dr. James B. Conant wrote in *The Atlantic Monthly* an article entitled "Wanted: American Radicals" in which he said:

> . . . The names of the predecessors of the European radicals are to be found on the lists of the Fabian Society of England of a generation back. The nearest approach to their ideals is to be seen in the miraculous Russian state.

Surely the head of a university should know that an English Radical was never a member of the Fabian society. English Radicals were opposed to bureaucracy. Their notion was: the less government, the better. It was the economic and political ideals of English Radicals—Priestley, Cartwright, and Paine—that were promulgated by the founders of the Republic.

Well, our Fabians had a merry time of it until the end of the war, when most of them decided to cast off the toga of the great Cunctator, because the Stalinites had suddenly become unpopular. Looking back it is astonishing to find that no one of importance uttered a warning note, not a word about the danger that threatened to overwhelm us.

There was no Edward Coke to curb our James I. There was no John Taylor of Caroline to remind him that

> . . . A constitutional expulsion of a stock-jobbing paper interest, in every shape, out of the national legislature, can alone recover the lost principles of a representative government, and save the nation from being owned—bought—and sold. . . .

There was no Jefferson to pronounce a word of warning. In 1782 the far-seeing Thomas said:

> . . . The public money and public liberty, intended to have been deposited with three branches of magistracy, but found inadvertently to be in the hands of one only, will soon be discovered to be sources of wealth and dominion to those who hold them. . . . They [the assembly] should look forward to a time, and that not a distant one, when a corruption in this, as in the country from which we derive our origin,

will have seized the heads of government, and be spread by
them through the body of the people; when they will purchase the voices of the people, and make them pay the
price. . . .

After nearly twenty years of trial and sorrow, we
find ourselves in the very chains the Founding Fathers
struck from their shins in 1776. The indictments set
down in the Declaration of Independence are strange to
read in this year of grace. There are two worth remembering that bear upon the present condition:

> He has made Judges dependent on his Will alone, for the
> tenure of their offices, and the amount and payment of their
> salaries.
> He has erected a multitude of New Offices, and sent
> hither swarms of Officers to harass our people, and eat out
> their substance.

So the judgment of Holmes, given in the *Truax v.
Corrigan* case, that "rights of property and the liberty
of the individual must be remolded, from time to time,
to meet the changing needs of society," has, in practice,
landed us back on the Hanoverian shore. That is a
political achievement performed by no other State in
history.

Now the most sinister changes in the Constitution
were insidiously brought about by resorting to the old
trick of creating an emergency. This I dealt with in
Sociocratic Escapades. I then asked: "What is an emergency?" After giving the definition of the term and
describing the conditions that prevailed from 1929 to
1934, I wrote:

> . . . There must be a limit to the duration of a sudden and
> unexpected crisis, unless one concedes that a political emer-
> gency has no end for those who use it for a cloak under
> which ulterior motives and secret policies are carried into
> effect.

It is difficult to formulate a law that would give to a
constitutional head of a State such power that he alone

would decide when an emergency had arisen and that he could take measures to deal with it without consulting the Congress. For it is not possible to imagine such a model of rectitude and wisdom as one mere man for a task Solomon himself feared to undertake. He had to call upon the Lord to help him: "I am but a little child: I know not how to go out or come in."

In our case, it was not the Lord that helped to give the Executive such powers as a Hitler or a Mussolini arrogated; it was Congress, the representives of a free democracy. It was merely a political expedient purchased by patronage; a party dodge—to use the old phrase for such nefarious practices. Congress shirked its responsibilities for a mess of pottage. One senator publicly declared: "I am for the New Deal because my State has received millions from the national Treasury." Of course! Caesar did the same thing to make himself popular.

The pretext of an emergency for bolstering a crumbling administration is an ancient device and was practiced frequently by Greek and Roman politicians. In *Sociocratic Escapades*, I wrote:

> To say nothing of the gold standard emergency, the veterans' emergency, the Muscle Shoals emergency, and the numerous other ones which cropped up in the night before the administration was a year old, we have had the silver emergency, the building emergency, the power emergency, and no one knows how many others will appear upon the political scene before we are many months older. There is no doubt at all in the minds of some people who enthusiastically supported the Roosevelt policies a few months ago, that this is the one and only "emergency" administration that has ever directed affairs in this country.

Panic legislation was the order of the day, and the reasons given by the Chief Executive and his myrmidons for the revolutionary measures were so extravagant, so utterly improbable, that the wonder of it was that majorities in the House and Senate were mustered for them. Quintus Fabius Maximus would have broken out in sweat had he been there to see our Fabians, in and out of the executive mansion, exceeding the speed limit in racing on to destroy the vital provisions of the Constitution.

The Coming American Revolution, the title of a book by George Soule, was on the doorstep after twelve months' work in Congress. After the trials and the tribulations of the first term of the Fabian administration, it began to dawn on some people that a real revolution was taking place to save us from an imaginary one. Before the end of the wars in Europe, in the Pacific, in Asia, and other spheres of interest, many of our people contracted hectic fever and found themselves so weakened by the revolution at home and slaughter abroad that they forgot to consider the plight of their minds when peace day was reached. Potsdam caused a relapse so serious that it is now prophesied by political seers that we shall have to fight another war to save the bit of civilization that survived the last one.

The Korean emergency saved us from a trade depression, and postponed, *sine die*, the Russian emergency. Meanwhile, the brave ally at the Kremlin has become a public nuisance, and no Fabian has a word to say in his defense. Quite the reverse! Indeed, many of his ardent supporters have sworn they were never affiliated with the ideals of the hero of Stalingrad. It is a topsy-turvy world we live in, but for changeability, it cannot be compared with the topsy-turvy minds of our Fabians.

Then came a period when many of our quasi-Socialists committed intellectual suicide. In some cases, philosophic hara-kiri was contemplated. I have a list of ten or twelve Fabians, very sanguine New Dealers, who are now qualifying for admission to the Upper House of Torydom.

The investigations into un-American activities have already exposed a sinister attempt by trusted servants of the State to change the system of government. But why did Congress wait until the house was burning before calling the fire brigade? There was evidence enough before the second administration of the Fabians was elected to show that our Guy Fawkeses were all set to put the light to the gunpowder to blow the Constitution to smithereens. The evidence can be found in a score of books published in the period 1933-36. It was not then investigated by Congress because there were emergencies, and the ruling power was Fabian.

Now it may be advanced that it is good political strategy to use expedient measures to gain a principle. The Fabian idea, as expressed by the English writers of that school, is to reach Socialism increment by increment. But in the English debates during the General Elections of 1910, it was found that no principle was formulated, and that the conception of the term Socialism was not accepted by those Fabians who were then masquerading as Liberal candidates.

Constitutional Radicals, opposed to bureaucratic government, decided that political Fabians had no principle to declare. Perhaps they knew that taking theory, based upon a principle, into the political arena was not unlike leading an ox into an abattoir.

Trade depressions and wars furnish the opportunities for political Socialists to set up dictatorships. An emergency is an excuse for suspending the provisions of the Constitution, and once Congress abandons its control and surrenders its powers to the executive, it is not likely that the unrestricted ruler will, without struggle, divest himself of the authority he has enjoyed. Power corrupts, and every newspaper reader knows now the infamy of corrupt officials of the State and how low the moral notion of a public trust has fallen since Laski began to inculcate his very young pupils with notions of a utopia for Fabians.

XIII

The Breeding Ground of Communism

THERE IS NO POLITICAL OR SOCIAL REASON WHY ANY intelligent man should blink the fact that America and, perhaps, Western Europe are engaged in a crusade to overcome what is called Communism. Therein lies a danger which may threaten to destroy that objective. A Third World War, we should know by now, cannot possibly be waged by a free community. If the power to be conquered is completely totalitarian, the power that opposes it must be totalitarian too. The conduct of World War II should be sufficient lesson for us to realize, before we enter upon another, that the strict disciplines of the enemy, exercised for many years before the conflict took place, brought speedy results, to the discomfiture of the democracies.

Therefore, it behooves us to ask ourselves whether piecemeal preparations for a third war will save us from the immense power of our enemy. It may seem strange to the ordinary man that the free and easy methods of the democracies in days of peace should be sacrificed before war is declared, and that the United States and Great Britain should institute, even in a cold war, disciplines that are different from those of Soviet Russia only in the label it is convenient for us to put upon them.

Already serious thinkers are reminding us of the suffering we have had to endure for over thirty years.

It is well that this should be pointed out, but whether it will have any effect on politicians or their electorates is a matter that cannot be determined. There is no Gallup poll that might help us to ascertain the thought of the people on this subject. Moreover, it must be conceded that public opinion today is made, to a great extent, by the last message broadcast over the radio.

There seems to be a feeling abroad that the majority do not look for a Third World War. We may have a few officials and laymen who think that the best way out of the mess is to have what is called "a preventive war," but this is an idea that is quite foreign to the mass of people. However, it is an extremely dangerous view to hold, particularly when it is advocated by a prominent member of a cabinet.

There are factors in the present phase of affairs, which should be pondered deeply before we commit ourselves to an ideological crusade, in which we should have to adopt the strict disciplines of the enemy. One factor is the political significance of war as an industry. He would be a short-sighted man who was blind to the fact that the rumors of war alone are almost sufficient to accelerate the wheels of industry and to mop up the remnants of the unemployed. The draft, mobilization, and training of men for the various fighting services demand more and more munitions. Industry is speeded up to fill the maw of the devouring monster, war.

Another factor is the political situation of the parties: the call to arms neutralizes the opposition forces, and draws everyone into the net of political patriotism, in favor of the ruling administration. This means that the dividing line between political democracy and Communism, so thinly drawn by particularists, vanishes when Congress or Parliament determines the hour for the start of the conflict.

The most precious thing that remains for us to cherish in our system of government is the power of the electorate to petition legislators to make reforms for its

benefit. But this can only be exercised during a period
of peace. Once the declaration to fight has been made,
there is no opportunity whatever to ameliorate the
sufferings that are now endured, even in the freest
political democracy that can be imagined. Under totalitarian disciplines, which would have to be adopted,
one thing and one thing only would be of importance,
and that would be the general exertion to wage the war
to a successful military issue. "Victory!" would be the
insistent slogan all round the clock, and those who
would attempt to put forward claims that Congress
should deal with reforms long held in abeyance would
be looked upon as shirkers or defeatists. It was so during
the First World War and the Second, and such would
be the case in a Third World War. This precious power
of the electors would disappear, with no hope of its
being regained.

There is still another matter to be considered, and
that is the objective of such a conflict. It is held by
many that, if it begins it will be for the purpose of
protecting ourselves from Communism of the Soviet
brand. Whether this be a reasonable excuse for bringing
more suffering upon the world or not must be left to
the intelligence of those who are asked to fight and
support the forces. For twenty years after the Treaty of
Versailles, Communism was as firm a doctrine in Russia
as it is now. But no one suggested that it was a danger
to democracy. At least, no one thought of committing
any nation to an ideological crusade against it.

It may be pointed out that in the days of Napoleon
Bonaparte, republicanism was regarded with much of
the same horror as Communism is today. Yet, after the
ravages of Europe—long after Napoleon was sent to
St. Helena—republicanism had not been killed in France.
Before Pitt began his crusade against Napoleon, a form
of republicanism in the American colonies was looked
upon with loathing by George III and his ministers.
And after all the fighting, republicanism lived on, and

today any man who desires may read the Declaration of Independence and learn what it was all about.

Surely these examples show that you cannot shoot holes into an idea. Whether it be right or wrong is not the chief question, but it does mean that untold suffering was brought to the people and that the crusades failed. The objectives of makers of war are seldom reached. World War II began for the purpose of protecting the sovereignty of Poland against Hitler's assault. But very soon after Poland was overthrown, other aims had to be invented.

After six years of terrible suffering, it was admitted that the only objective that had been gained was a military victory, which placed Stalin so far west in Europe that he has ever since been a menace to the democracies. As for the defeat of dangerous ideologies, the war settled nothing. Indeed, it made matters worse for the politicians of the west, and now we are reaping the deadly fruits of their blunders and those of their unenlightened supporters. Our lot during the phase of the cold war has been bad enough.

The destruction to life and property in Europe, to say nothing of what it was in the rest of the world, was so enormous that the expenditure reached the amazing figure of a trillion and many billions of dollars. Today there are sad reports of homeless people suffering in lands to which we promised to bring peace and happiness. We are now informed that northern Africa, from Casablanca to the Nile, is seething with discontent, and that the distress of many of the natives is woeful in the extreme.

It may be asked what we have accomplished, when we are called upon to defray the cost of rehabilitating the peoples of countries that fought with us in the crusade of the Second World War. Surely, there is no more effective way of turning hungry men's minds to such a doctrine as Communism than a devastating war. War gave Lenin and Trotsky the opportunity to enter Russia and overthrow the Czarist régime. It also gave the opportunity to French Communists to gather strength in their country.

But the doctrine of the Soviets was rife in many countries before Neville Chamberlain gave the pledge of support of arms to Poland in March, 1939. War enlarges the field for the dissemination of the ideas of Communism. The doctrine of the Kremlin feeds upon suffering, material stint, "the slings and arrows of outrageous fortune" that hit the impoverished day by day and make the hope of a better morrow a thing of gloom.

What, then, might be done to protect the millions from the virus we all dread? Is it not a better way to rid ourselves of this menace by answering doctrine with doctrine? Have we not learned that it is not sufficient to tell the people what Stalin's Communism is in practice—an enslavement of the workers, a restriction of thought, and a deprivation of all spiritual attributes— in short, a slave system under the will of a bureau?

The intelligent workingman of a generation ago desired a clearer idea of what communism really is in theory than his fellow of today demands of our instructors. When discussions were held at the Cooper Union in New York over fifty years ago, the practice of debating doctrine against doctrine brought enlightenment to the audiences that attended the meetings. And that was at a time when there was little or no danger of Communists overturning the government of the United States and setting up a régime in Washington.

The proposals and conceptions of Communism were then analyzed by some of the shrewdest thinkers who lived in New York. And so convincing were the method and clarity of the exposition that the Communists made little or no progress. If some of those thinkers were here today, they would be amazed to know that people indulge in such nonsense as to believe that theoretical Communism is practiced in Soviet Russia.

It is difficult to understand the reasons for the fear of Soviet Communism (or what goes by that name), which has been implanted in the minds of our political mentors. There is no earthly chance of Russians in Moscow changing our system of government. If it is to be done, it will be effected by the so-called Communists in the United States.

Lenin, in *State and Revolution*, says:

> The essence of revolution is not that a new class shall govern by means of the old governmental machinery, but that it shall smash up this machinery and govern by means of a new machine. This is a fundamental idea of Marxism.

This seems to me to be clear enough. If the machinery of our government is to be smashed, it will be done by the electorate of the United States. No one knew that better than Lenin himself, for revolutions spring out of dire distress of the people in the State to which they belong. Therefore, the first step that should be taken to avoid such a catastrophe is to enlighten the people, so that they may force their legislators to redress their grievances.

Two years after the *Communist Manifesto* was published, there appeared in France a pamphlet called *The Law*. It was written by Frederic Bastiat, an economist and a deputy to the legislative assembly. A version of this famous work has recently been published by the Foundation for Economic Education. Every member of a legislative body in this country should get a copy of this booklet. Bastiat tells us that "The present-day delusion is an attempt to enrich everyone at the expense of everyone else; to make plunder universal under the pretense of organizing it."

He then goes on to show the labyrinths of the plunder system of government, and, strangely enough, they are those that we know only too well here in the United States. For he points out that tariffs, subsidies, progressive taxation, guaranteed jobs, minimum wages, the "right" to relief, and many other such fiscal by-ways into the pockets of the producer are all part of legal plunder and constitute Socialism.

Bastiat, having made good his case against the *Plunderbund* of government, called upon the people to refute the pernicious doctrine of Marx and Engels. He said:

> Now, since under this definition Socialism is a body of doctrine, what attack can be made against it other than a war of doctrine? If you find this socialistic doctrine to be false, absurd, and evil, then refute it. And the more false, the more absurd, and the more evil it is, the easier it will be to refute. Above all, if you wish to be strong, begin by rooting out every particle of Socialism that may have crept into your legislation. This will be no light task.

Refute it! That is what we have to do. It was difficult one hundred years ago, notwithstanding men like Bastiat in France, in Germany, and in England. Today it is easy. The only reason it is not done is that men are lazy, and will not take the trouble to study the question. Is it necessary to fight, to try to shoot holes into the idea? The notion is preposterous. Montalembert was accused of desiring to fight Socialism by the use of brute force. What was his reply? "The war that we must fight against Socialism must be in harmony with law, honor, and justice."

What is required today, is enlightenment. Our legislators seem to be no better informed than the people themselves. Neither from pulpit nor from rostrum has a clear statement been presented of what the ideologies are that they hear so much about. Our libraries contain hundreds of volumes by some of the world's keenest thinkers on Socialism and Communism. It may be doubted whether any well-known book of the past two centuries has been submitted to such closely reasoned analysis as *Das Kapital*. And, yet, we have instructors in our institutions of learning who reveal in their writings that they are ignorant of such works. It is not necessary to mention the authors of French and German volumes who have thoroughly dissected Marx's theory of surplus value and labor time. Two books which might be easily obtained in a well-ordered library are Professor Robert Flint's *Socialism* and Max Hirsch's *Democracy Versus Socialism.* In them the intelligent reader will find a complete reply to Marx.

But Socialists themselves have written many illuminating works that expose the fallacies of the authors of the *Communist Manifesto* and *Das Kapital.* These books should now engage the attention of all people who dread a Third World War, for they cover all the vexed questions that have arisen since Marx wrote his chief work.

Fifty years ago the thoroughgoing Communist accepted the following statement of the proposals and conceptions of Socialism and Communism: the State shall control all the means of production, distribution and exchange, *for the equal benefit of all;* and the State shall have power over persons, their faculties, and possessions. This was the theory accepted by State Socialists and Communists, who scorned to enter the political arena. The impossibility of putting such a scheme into practice did not concern them very much, for they were specifically interested in announcing an idea in opposition to the theories of Proudhon and Bakunin, the anarchists. No such theory has been put into practice in any country. Indeed, Stalinism is so far divorced from the original idea of Marx and Engels that it is impossible to understand how anything that is done in Russia can bear the label of Communism.

It might be asked how any sensible man could imagine that the proposals and conceptions of Socialism, as stated by Max Hirsch and Robert Flint, could be put into practice, once the omnipotent, bureaucratic State was set up. The impossibility of distributing the products of labor, *for the equal benefit of all*, turns the idea into an utter absurdity.

What goes by the name of Communism today is nothing more or less than bureaucratic control of the workers. They are slaves of the State, and Franz Oppenheimer, in his work called *The State*, proved conclusively that it (the State) "is the organization of the political means to exploit the economic means." Power over producers is the bureaucratic aim.

The fear of the power of the Russian leaders to spread the doctrine of Communism abroad is a recent one. Not so long ago they were valuable allies and no one seemed to be much afraid of the system of government they had inaugurated. In this war against ideology, it also should not be forgotten that years before the names of Lenin, Trotsky, and Stalin became current in the press, the doctrines of Communism and Socialism were preached freely in this country as well as in Great Britain. For at least ten years before the First World War this writer was debating these questions.

As recently, in this generation, as the beginning of the Roosevelt régime, there were coteries in our institutions of learning that advocated a system similar to the one practiced in Russia. Many of our intelligentsia then declared that they were opposed to the capitalistic system and held strong views as to the necessity of inculcating students with the ideas of Fabianism, as expressed by the late Harold Laski. There were, in our midst, hot gospellers of the creed of Socialism of sufficient influence to make an impression upon young minds, before anyone thought of starting a violent crusade against Soviet Russia.

All the nostrums of so-called reform, that flutter about in the minds of politicians, are tainted with the desire to perpetuate the system of taxation of wealth, so long as the people will permit them to do so. They will promise reform of it, but even the sincerest finds, once he becomes a member of a legislature, he is hedged about by a thousand and one other claims that crowd in upon his desire for the lifting of burdens. He becomes a victim of the system, and he must either lend himself to the surge of the political tide or resign. How many do so, when they know that there is not the slightest chance of positive reform being brought to the notice of Congress or Parliament? The demands for expenditure on the great services, as sops and doles, are so vast that reform of the system of the taxation of wealth seems an impossible goal to be reached.

In all this mêlée, we overlook many features that might be lost entirely if a Third World War took place. We should guard closely the political and social opportunities that have not yet been filched from us.

The history of the past 150 years reveals as clearly as possible the fact that there is no surer way of preparing the field for the seeds of socialistic notions than war. The condition of Europe, from the time of Waterloo to the publication of the *Communist Manifesto*—a full generation—had not recovered from the ravages of the Napoleonic Wars. The year 1848 was one of revolutions and riots in the principal countries of Europe. Communist societies sprang up in all the chief cities. Wherever there was concentrated poverty, there were missioners who preached the creed of Socialism. The literature of the period, from the year 1848 to the outbreak of the Franco-German War, contains hundreds of pages of accounts of outbreaks of disorder, occasioned by the discontent of the people.

After the failure of Louis Blanc's national workshops in Paris, Victor Hugo declared them to have proved a fatal experiment, and he wrote:

> . . . The wealthy idler we already know; you have created a person a hundred times more dangerous both to himself and to others—the *pauper* idler. At this very moment England sits smiling by the side of the abyss into which France is falling.

During the siege of Paris the Communists turned loose, and the streets ran with blood. Egon Friedell, in *A*

Cultural History of the Modern Age, tells in brief the story of the Commune in 1870:

> . . . Only after two months' fighting did MacMahon succeed in entering the city at the head of regular troops. The "bloody week," in which he suppressed the insurrection in a savage war of barricades, was the most ghastly butchery of civilians in modern history. It was just at this moment that the Chinese embassy arrived in Paris. Excuses were offered, but the head of the mission replied: "No need for apology. You are young, you Occidentals, you have practically no history. It is always thus: siege and commune, that is the normal history of mankind."

So it goes. War brings discontent and disunion. People made desolate by the loss of their dear ones, the destruction of their property, and the violation of their homes, turn to any creed they think will alleviate their distress. Why there should be any doubt about this, no one pretends to say. The literature on the subject is vast, and most of it can be found in the large public libraries. A work that might help our instructors to enlighten us is *This Age of Ours*, published in 1895. The writer of this essay has an autographed copy from its author, Dr. Charles Hermann Leibbrand, who was a journalist in Manchester. Many well-known personages of the period, such as Lecky, Herbert Spencer, the Duke of Argyll, John Tyndall, and Professor Froude, read it and corresponded with the author about his views.

It contains a series of essays on the most significant political problems of that time, and in looking at its pages today (notwithstanding its fallacies, exaggerations, and dogmatism), one realizes that a story runs through it all that might be read with intellectual benefit by our mentors. Leibbrand was something of a prophet, but I doubt very much that he would admit, if he were here now, that he ever imagined the Communism of which he wrote would assume such a shape as it has taken on and become the dreaded menace of all free-thinking people.

Communism (or Socialism) is not a doctrine that has sprung from the minds of the impoverished. They have never been makers of creeds. From the earliest times of discontent and revolt, they have been the prey of those who desire political change and bureaucratic power. Only comparatively few in any period of which we have record have formulated socialistic doctrines or communistic creeds. Literary men have indulged in this recreation and have left us many of their works. The writers in this country who have pursued this avocation are familiar, and it is not necessary to name them. Looking back over my life in America, which extends now to seventy-two years, I cannot remember reading a single book on Socialism or Communism that was written by an impoverished workingman.

Most of the writing done in England during a like period, came from the pens of well-known authors—Sidney Webb, George Bernard Shaw, H. G. Wells, and several others who "never wielded a pick or an ax nor pushed mortar in a wheelbarrow." Their hands were not horny. Ink stains were the only blemish that industry made upon them. Moreover, it is doubtful whether their books on these subjects were read by the people the authors thought should be led into a collectivist Elysium. During my debates in England with Socialists and Social Democrats, I seldom heard of a workingman who read the essays of the Fabian literati. Therefore it cannot be said that knowledge of these creeds is possessed by the mass of workers. It is discontent, not knowledge of these doctrines, that is the chief cause of the revolt of the masses.

Looking over the past century and a half, it is a mighty problem to try to explain how intelligent people today can ignore the fact that war is a breeding ground of Communism. Think of what happened in all European countries after the First World War. The imagination need not be overwrought to ascertain the change of ideas in nearly all political parties after the Treaty of

Versailles. The Labor party in Great Britain lost its Radical-Liberal significance and became a Fabian-Socialistic one. We know what happened in Germany and how the gospel of Lenin was changed when Stalin became dictator at the Kremlin.

After the Second World War, a Socialist government was elected in Great Britain. If history does not repeat itself, war after war, it most assuredly takes on similar features. It is the same thing under perhaps a different name, but the cause of the change is discontent and disunion. The aim of the preacher against the system that makes for war never varies, and the choice of audience to whom he preaches his panacea is unalterable.

It is well to be reminded of the dangers inherent in our war policies. Scarcely a day passes when we notice some prominent personage of British or of European origin who warns us to take heed while we have time and opportunity to deal with politicians. Bertrand (Lord) Russell, in an article in *The New York Times Magazine*, September 3, 1950, tells us:

> There is only too much reason to fear that Western civilization, if not the whole world, is likely in the near future to go through a period of immense sorrow and suffering and pain—a period during which, if we are not careful to remember them, the things that we are attempting to preserve may be forgotten in bitterness and poverty and disorder. . . .

Russell goes straight to the point—"immense sorrow and suffering and pain" are the penalties of strife. But do our legislatures realize it? Do they know that in fighting Communism with deadly weapons, they are, in all likelihood, plowing the field in which the nostrums of Socialism and Communism will take root? Do the churches know what "immense sorrow and suffering and pain" have done in the past to turn men away from religion? George Savile, the Marquis of Halifax, as far back as the days of William of Orange, said: "Religion is the foundation of Government; without it man is an

abandoned creature, one of the worst beasts Nature has
produced.''

Russell is imbued with "a new hope for mankind.''
He looks for it in the advancement of science turned to
peaceful pursuits, and tells us:

> The hope cannot be realized unless the causes of present
> evils are understood. But it is the hope that needs to be
> emphasized. Modern man is master of his fate. What he suffers
> he suffers because he is stupid or wicked, not because it is
> nature's decree. Happiness is his if he will adopt the means
> that lie ready to his hands.

Many such expressions could be quoted, but alas, few
are to be found in the works recently published by our
authors. Professor J. W. Gough of Oriel College, Oxford,
who has written a very interesting work, *John Locke's
Political Philosophy* (Oxford, 1950), is also conscious of
the dangers that we run, and in dealing with the principles of the British Constitution, he advises his country-
men to respect them instead of abandoning them:

> Otherwise, although we may profess to eschew totalitar-
> ianism, we may, when it is too late, have cause to regret the
> disappearance of the safeguards against arbitrary power
> which our ancestors regarded as one of their chief blessings.

Our legislators cannot have it both ways. They cannot
destroy Communism by fighting those who have adopted
it as a political system without creating conditions that
will give it a new birth. Belligerent crusades have ever
failed to reach their objective. The crusades of Godefroy
de Bouillon and Richard I ended disastrously. Dr. Ernest
Barker, the historian, tells us: "The crusades may be
written down as a failure. They ended not in the occupa-
tion of the east by the Christian west, but in the con-
quest of the west by the Mohammedan east.''

This article may have been written in vain. It may be
too late to advise another way of dealing with the
menace. War is the only subject that precludes the

possibility of debate, with the aim of mutual understanding. In all channels of man's thought and activity, the most difficult problems can be resolved by the opposing disputants meeting face to face. It is possible, in such crises, for an arbitrator to assist in bringing the parties to agreement.

In war this is not so. The settlement of the dispute is left to the politicians, and the record of their work, so far, deprives us of any hope for the future. In this respect, it is only necessary to refer to the blunders that were made at Versailles and at Potsdam. These have been condemned by the shrewdest minds who have examined them. Small wonder Lord Russell is alarmed. There might be a gleam of hope if the churches would perform the duties incumbent upon them and begin to enlighten their congregations on the real issue, making them understand the advice of Ecclesiastes: "Wisdom is better than weapons of war."

XIV

What Is
"Equality of Opportunity"?

SOCRATES WAS A STICKLER FOR CLEAR DEFINITIONS. WHO can read *The Republic* and fail to enjoy his method of making his friends explain the meaning of the words they used that day they were gathered at the Piraeus, when they began their search for justice? The quest would have been fruitless if, at each step taken in the discussion, he had not insisted on clarifying the meaning of leading terms. Cicero, too, was strict about the necessity of defining economic and political ideas in a way so simple that his hearers understood what was meant. His declaration on natural law is an example of the care he took to make his meaning clear.

Marcus Aurelius was another who asked for precise definition. His advice is worth quoting:

> Make for thyself a definition or description of the thing which is presented to thee, so as to see distinctly what kind of a thing it is, in its substance, in its nudity, in its complete entirety, and tell thyself its proper name, and the names of the things of which it has been compounded, and into which it will be received.

These are precepts to be followed if we would know the exact meanings of terms. From the men who laid them down so long ago we gather that conversation was no less difficult then than it is now. Indeed, Plato's work, *The Republic*, will forever remain the outstanding example of the confusion in men's thought and how hard it is to make them understand that words and phrases must have particular meanings, if the time given to controversy is not to be misspent.

A few years ago, at a dinner party, held at the house of a physicist—a Nobel prize winner—one of the leading sociologists of the country asked, "What is to take the place of the capitalistic system?" The question was addressed to an economist, but before he could reply, the physicist put in, "What *is* the capitalistic system?"

The rest of the evening was taken up with an argument about the meaning of the phrase "capitalistic system," and so different were the ideas of the people at the table about it that the time passed without the original question being answered.

Socrates was perhaps the only philosopher who succeeded in making his disputants realize that they would get nowhere in their controversy about justice unless they agreed upon clear definitions of words. All through the centuries, down to our own day, we have had countless illustrations of the futility of attempting to determine what men mean by their leading terms unless, at the outset of the discussion, they agree upon precise definitions of the principal concepts.

Roger Bacon, the great Franciscan mathematician of the thirteenth century, said: "The mixture of those things by speech which are by nature divided is the mother of all error."

How strange it is that so little is done in the institutions of learning to enlighten the students about this necessary study. It is fundamental to a proper understanding of discourse. Yet, some of our modern philosophers, politicians, and economists reveal in their writings that they have not given due consideration to these matters. They are often as guilty of defects in expression as men were at any time.

One has only to think of the term laissez faire, as it has been used since the days of Archdeacon Cunningham, to know that this is so. The industrial system, often called the capitalistic system, is frequently described as one of laissez faire. However, when it is pointed out that there has never been, in any political civilization, a period of no restriction, thinking men realize that the term is misapplied. A free industrial system in a complex civilization has never been known, and since the days of the so-called Industrial Revolution, neither Great Britain nor any European country has been without restrictive laws which interfere with production and commerce. The confusion in the minds of students, caused by the misuse of this term, is responsible for much of the misunderstanding so widespread among Fabians and many sociologists.

The Physiocrats, who advocated an economic system of laissez faire, were a clear-thinking body of men. Henry Dunning Macleod, in his book, *Elements of Economics* (1881), described their doctrine and the industrial goal they had in view. It would serve a useful purpose if our mentors would prescribe a course in economic fundamentals that would include the study of the system advocated by the Physiocrats.

In his very interesting work, *The Growth of English Industry and Commerce in Modern Times* (1903), Dr. Cunningham repeatedly uses the term laissez faire, but nowhere does he explain what it really means. François Quesnay announced the doctrine in his work, *Le Droit Naturel* (1768), an inquiry into natural rights. It goes to the basis of man's urge to satisfy his desires and needs with the least exertion. It is a demand for freedom to produce the commodities that are necessary for his well-being. One of the clearest statements to be found upon the idea of the Physiocrats is that of Henry George, in *The Science of Political Economy*, Book II, Chapter IV, in which he translates and defines the motto of Quesnay: *"Laissez faire, laissez aller,"* as "A fair field and no favor."

It was not until long after the enclosure acts had depopulated the countrysides of England and driven men into the towns that the term laissez faire was applied to industry. But at no time since the discovery of coal and steam has there been such a condition as "a fair field and no favor." Restrictive industrial laws and the taxation of wealth had been in vogue since the days of the Stuarts. However, the so-called capitalistic system could not have raised its grimy edifices so speedily (when the machine driven by steam superseded the old village system of handicraft), had not enclosures supplied the labor market with an abundance of men who had no alternative. Indeed, it was a denial of laissez faire which produced a capitalism that throve on low-paid labor.

Quesnay and his colleagues did not envisage industrial conditions such as those that sprang into being after the discovery of coal and steam. He died in 1774, and the inventions of Watt, Hargreaves, and Arkwright were then in their infancy. It was not easy for those born fifty or sixty years later to find a perspective that would enable them to view the sequence of events that led to the Hungry Forties and the destitution rife in the manufacturing towns. Moreover, Quesnay could not know that an economic revolution was progressing covertly in England, with the object of despoiling the free laborers of the common fields and turning them adrift to crowd into urban districts in search of work.

According to Frederick Clifford's *A History of Private Bill Legislation* (1885), 3,511,814 acres of land were enclosed by private bills in the eighteenth century. But this figure is only the extent of the areas declared in the bills. As for enclosures and depopulation by force, such means for territorial aggrandizement had been taken ever since the days of John of Gaunt.

Quesnay's economic theory of dealing with the first factor in production, land—the passive factor, the created one—was philosophically sound, and in it lay the attribute of freedom to produce, equality of opportunity.

This period—the century and a half from 1700 to 1850—deserves a new, thorough treatment, now that we have so much fresh material, much of it discovered by John Hammond. But it will serve no educative purpose to survey it from our present-day vantage point. The recorder might begin with James E. Thorold Rogers' book, *Six Centuries of Work and Wages*, and trace the thread of this most terrible of all revolutions, stretching from the end of the thirteenth century, when a serf held twelve acres of arable, down to our own day, when the great mass are landless wage slaves.

In a review of Henry Steele Commager's book, *The American Mind* (1950), Joseph Wood Krutch quotes from it:

> What populism and progressivism, the new freedom and the New Deal, meant in terms of political philosophy was the final repudiation of laissez-faire and the explicit recognition of government as a social welfare agency.

Here in America an industrial system of laissez faire has not existed since the birth of trade unionism. Protective tariffs, factory laws, social legislation, and trade union demands for higher nominal wage and fewer working hours are contrary to all the ideas that were held by the Physiocrats. It is not a question of whether these expedients were necessary to ameliorate the economic distress. The consequence of such legislation shows clearly that as more of these measures are put upon the statute book, more are required to bolster them. Nothing has been done to provide man with an alternative to entering the labor market, and we have seen the dollar he earns (when he gets a chance to work) shrink in purchasing power. Moreover, all the labor-saving aids produced by science and invention tend to make life harder for him.

Another word employed loosely by politicians and editors is "radical." If the members of the famous Radical Club of Boston could know how it is used

today, they would be amazed. Every member of that
unique society was an individualist, whether he were a
Whig, a Democrat, or a Republican. How this term
has been twisted to cover the nostrums of Socialists and
Communists no one pretends to say. In England and in
this country it was in use long before the days of Marx
and Engels.

The Oxford Dictionary gives a satisfactory definition
of it, and there is no excuse whatever for its being misapplied. It means "root," and an English Radical of the
eighteenth century was a man who desired the restoration of the Constitution; the abolition of landlordism;
and the reestablishment and reaffirmation of "the law
and custom of the land."

This claim appears occasionally in philosophical and
political tracts since the days of Edward the Confessor,
though it is scarcely noticed by the Radicals of the
school of Grote, Mill, and Molesworth. Thomas Paine
was a Radical, and so was Thomas Jefferson. Only one
who is not particular about his definitions could use it
to designate political and social nostrums that are as
superficial as those in vogue today.

How often we notice now in the speeches of politicians
and in the essays of men directing the fortunes of our
institutions of learning the phrase "equality of opportunity." A former President of this country frequently
inserted it in his fireside chats, but it was left to the
discretion of the listeners as to what he meant by it.
Whether he referred to it in a social sense or a political
or economic one, none could gather from the context in
which it was embedded.

What is implied by it would certainly make a great
difference to the understanding of those whose opportunity to earn a decent living is thwarted by restrictive
laws. For so many people it seems to be somewhat like
the blessed word Mesopotamia—high sounding and of
merely decorative purpose; a literary boss or a bit of
chiselled foliage for a capital.

Many years ago a popular archbishop delivered a sermon in which he called for a system of equality of opportunity. Afterwards, some of his parishioners wanted to know what he meant by the phrase. He explained that he used it in an economic sense, a desire for the people to have access to land, which is the basis of their existence.

The controversy that arose from this explanation impressed the archbishop with the fact that those in his see who, in their domains, held sway over natural resources were not inclined to part with their acres. Needless to say, the archbishop dropped the subject and returned to sermons which in no way disturbed the economic notions of his well-to-do parishioners. A newspaper commenting upon the controversy said that it was better for church dignitaries to stick to sin, schism, and squalor. Within the church there could be very little controversy about these daily problems.

In an interview published in *The New York Times Magazine*, March 5, 1950, Dr. A. W. Griswold, the new president of Yale University, said:

> By democracy I mean a political society in which the greatest possible measure of justice implicit in the phrase *equal opportunity* is combined with the greatest possible measure of freedom and encouragement for the individual to develop his own talent, initiative and moral responsibility . . . .

Here we find it in a context which gives us the impression that the speaker has a definite idea of what the phrase signifies, and perhaps he took it for granted that there would be no doubt in the mind of the reader as to its application. He may have thought no one would so misunderstand the use to which he put it as to imagine it had a political or social significance.

In a democracy where adult suffrage is established, we are supposed to be on a basis of equality of opportunity, so far as voting goes. Here there is no such privilege as that which was enjoyed by the plural voter in Great Britain up until a few years ago. One adult, one vote, is the basis of the franchise in this country. But after the voting is over and the candidates have been elected to the legislatures, the equality of opportunity of the elector ceases to be a determining factor, and through lack of further interest the legislators are left to themselves to conduct the affairs of the nation. The daily papers are full of instances of privilege, nepotism, and graft, and the investigating committees organized to deal with abuse are so many that it is difficult to sustain interest in their proceedings. Therefore, it might be said that the electors' equality of opportunity in political affairs comes to an end when the poll closes on election day.

Now in social affairs there cannot be equality of opportunity for all in a democracy. In the first place, it is not in the nature of man—nor, indeed, in that of woman—to desire it. The first difficulty would be in determining from which stratum the move should be made—from below, up, or from up, down. It is only necessary to walk through the neighborhoods of a medium-sized town and notice the places where the various sections of the community live to be convinced that social equality of opportunity is impossible under this system. There are supposed to be no class distinctions in the land of the free. That may be so in theory, but it is certainly not so in practice.

Some time ago a critic of the system remarked that only at baseball games, race meetings, and prize fights does one see the classes mix on a democratic basis. In the main, this is true, and to a certain extent it is true of such sporting events in Europe. Yet, we have our special enclosures and sections in grandstands for those who can afford to pay high prices for their seats. Money talks, and though we despise such social divisions as upper classes, middle classes, and lower classes, we realize that the purse has much the same significance everywhere; the amount of income only too often denotes the social line of demarcation between one section of the community and another.

President Griswold tells us he is in favor of "the greatest possible measure of justice implicit in the phrase *equal opportunity*." What makes his declaration somewhat unique is that he associates the term justice with "freedom and encouragement for the individual to develop his own talent, initiative and moral responsibility."

There have been notions just as confused about the meaning of the term "justice" as there have been about the phrase "equality of opportunity." I presume Socrates would say, if he were at Yale, that equality of opportunity was synonymous with justice. But who is prepared to create a State such as Socrates had in mind? Some years ago I made a composite definition of justice as it is described in *The Republic:*

> Justice is the institution of a natural order in which a man can produce food, buildings, and clothing for himself, removing not a neighbour's landmark, practising one thing only, the thing to which his nature is best adapted, doing his own business, not being a busybody, not taking what is another's nor being deprived of what is his own, having what is his own, and belongs to him, interfering not with another, so that he may set in order his own inner life, and be his own master, his own law, and at peace with himself.

These ideas may be gained from the debates that took place on the occasion of the festival of Bendis, the Thracian Artemis. The event—almost forgotten now—was one of the most important recorded in history, and it would be well for those who are interested in a bureaucratic State to return to *The Republic* and learn once more about the ideas held by wise men centuries before the beginning of the Christian Era. It would take a book of many pages to follow the lines of thought inspired by Socrates.

Think of the work of the jurisconsults of Rome. In the *Institutes of Justinian* it is laid down that "he is just who gives to each what belongs to him." The Fathers

of the Church saw to the heart of this idea and clearly
differentiated between land and property. Down through
the Dark Ages, into the Middle Ages, and as near our
time as Richard Hooker and Joseph Butler, thinkers
have expressed themselves in the terms set forth by
Socrates.

However, we live in a workaday world, and we seem
not to be interested in philosophical abstractions. We
are practical people, and much of our thought is given
to the making of the hydrogen bomb and the question
of who will drop it first. Science has taken possession
of the field of ideas, and now the physicists together
with the laymen are victims of the political system in
which we live, for the present.

It is to be hoped that President Griswold will have a
fair field and no favor, and we shall watch with deep
interest his pilgrmage of peace in a society that is in
sad need of his assistance.

Philosophers and jurists, since the days of Plato and
Cicero, have interpreted natural law in an economic
sense, and their commentators—at least from the time
of Aquinas to John Locke—have promulgated the idea
that man has a right to use the earth, which is necessary
for his subsistence. Equality of opportunity, therefore,
means nothing less than equal rights to use land because
man is a land animal and cannot live or work without
it.

There should be no doubt of this in the mind of a
cultivated American because when this Republic was
founded, many men expressed themselves clearly upon
this matter. St. George Tucker and John Taylor followed
the Lockian tradition closely and expressed their notions
of natural right in the same downright manner as Coke
and Blackstone. Tucker says: "All men being by nature
equal, in respect to their rights, no man nor set of men,
can have any natural, or inherent right, to rule over the
rest."

It would be well for some of our latter-day exponents of economic and political affairs to return to the writings of the men of the Revolutionary era. An excellent work for students is *American Interpretations of Natural Law*, by Benjamin Fletcher Wright, Jr. Though it may be late in the day to do anything of a practical nature to restore economic rights, it would do no harm if educators of influence in our institutions of learning renewed acquaintance with the thought of men who laid the philosophical basis for the structure of this Republic.

A fascinating study for a man who thinks and writes is to notice the accretions of definitions given to simple terms since Johnson compiled his dictionary. It is difficult to keep pace with the various shades and meanings that creep upon a word like ivy on a wall. The more we learn, the more need for a lexicon.

Some years ago I received from the great-nephew of Archbishop Trench a very unusual present—a copy of the twenty-seventh edition of *On The Study of Words* (1st ed., 1851). The Archbishop wrote it just about one hundred years ago, and when I was a boy, scholars in the higher forms were reminded of it frequently in the courses in English literature.

Alas, it is out of date, and only philologists would derive pleasure from a study of it. We live in an age when great masses of people so little understand the metrical beauty of the King James Version of the New Testament that it has to be rewritten. It is a sad commentary on the schooling now given to the people, for it should be remembered that for several generations the poor spelled out the sentences and memorized many of them. What was understood then by the poor who, in a great measure had to educate themselves, cannot be read now with understanding by those who have had the benefits of higher education.

The interview of President Griswold in *The New York Times* gives hope of a better day. He certainly expresses himself freely. As the head of an institution of learning in this country, he is to be welcomed for the courage revealed in this proclamation. To announce a desire to initiate a "measure of justice implicit in the phrase *equal opportunity*" presages a new life for the university whose future will be under his guidance. If he will now dissipate any doubts as to the significance of the terms he uses, he may succeed in a mission to make us "pacemakers in a free world."

I would remind him of the closing words Trench wrote to the preface of his book:

> . . . A meditative man cannot refrain from wonder, when he digs down to the deep thought lying at the root of many a metaphorical term, employed for the designation of spiritual things, even of those with regard to which professing philosophers have blundered grossly; and often it would seem as though rays of truth, which were still below the intellectual horizon, had dawned upon the imagination as it was looking up to heaven. Hence they who feel an inward call to teach and enlighten their countrymen, should deem it an important part of their duty to draw out the stores of thought which are already latent in their native language, to purify it from the corruptions which Time brings upon all things, and from which language has no exemption, and to endeavour to give distinctness and precision to whatever in it is confused, or obscure, or dimly seen.

How we are to become "pacemakers in a free world" is not clearly explained. No one would say the world is free at the present time. Indeed, it would be hard to convince a laboring man that he is free to take a line that differs fundamentally from the one prescribed by his government or by his union. Our actions in this country are circumscribed, not only by the greatest bureaucracy the world has known, but by the injustices of the system of taxation, which makes equality of opportunity a goal that lies far below the horizon.

Before we can change the systems of States in Europe and Asia, we must alter the conditions that hamper our efforts here to make ourselves free in an economic sense. But how this is to be done by communities that have no knowledge of fundamental economics is a conundrum that cannot be answered. Although in the newsprints day after day we read about economics, we do not gather that the writers have the slightest idea of first principles.

Economics—housekeeping—is an elastic term, but it has been stretched so much since the days of Marx that the men who founded this Republic would not recognize it. An advertisement in the business section of a newspaper recently offered schooling in the "economics of bookkeeping and auditing."

This is an instance of how far we have departed from the root meaning of the words we use. Therefore, if we are to understand one another, it is necessary to clear away the accretions that have gathered about terms, so that the confusions of thought will be dissipated, and men will know what is meant by the appeals made to inspire them, in an effort to reach a goal of economic security.

XV

The Gospel of Justice

LONG CENTURIES HAVE PASSED SINCE INDIVIDUALISTS AND
Socialists began their search for an Elysium in which
humankind might settle down, live in peace, and enjoy
an abundance of the good things of earth. So far, their
efforts have failed signally to impress the tenants of
lands east, west, north, and south, that they might aid
in the adventure and plan a future for themselves and
their heirs that would be less toilsome than the system
which they now endure.

Perhaps one of the chief reasons for the apathy of
mortals to making a change for the better is that they
are still addicted to the blood-and-grime business of
war. And now that threats and rumors of strife are
politically necessary to keep labor and capital employed
in making munitions, the industrial victims of the State
imagine war loaves are larger than peace rolls, and
preparations for a fight will insure for them a steady
job, enabling them to pay the installments on their
cars, radios, and television sets.

It may be that such a system is, to the artisan, an
Elysium—the best that can be hoped for in this world
of confusion and turmoil; and that it is safe to think
that it will last, at any rate, until he is eligible for an
old-age pension.

The nineteenth century was not alone in producing
men who really believed that most of the troubles which
beset their fellows were economically unnecessary. As
long ago as the days of Pindar, the Greek poet, there

was an idea abroad that there had been a time when men knew a pleasant existence. In the *Isles of the Blessed* we learn of that happy condition:

> They till not the ground, they plow not the wave,
>   They labor not, never! oh, never!
> Not a tear do they shed, not a sigh do they heave;
>   They are happy for ever and ever!

Even so late in the classical period as the time of Justinian, Roman jurists held the notion that conditions for humankind were better in the days when no one spoke of progress than they were under the rule of imperial Rome. Indeed, it is easy to trace this notion all through the Pentateuch down to the time of Jesus, through medieval days, during the Renaissance, terminating with the great announcement of the Prophet of San Francisco.

Henry George was imbued with such a high ideal that I sometimes think he might have been looking over the shoulder of Alexander Pope when he wrote the lines:

> All crimes shall cease, and ancient fraud shall fail,
> Returning Justice lift aloft her scale,
> Peace o'er the world her olive wand extend,
> And white-robed Innocence from heaven descend.

The rosy hopes of modern economic idealists began to wither toward the end of the last century. The imperial policies of the six leading powers of the world turned men's attention away from the things to be bettered at home, and launched them into wars waged for the ownership of natural resources of backward lands. The Cuban war, the Boer War, and the Russo-Japanese War were conflicts that foreshadowed the outbreak of the First World War.

The exploitation of territories rich in diamonds and gold, tin and tungsten, rubber and fuel, were El Dorados for the concessionaires who, without mercy, slaughtered thousands of natives and enslaved the survivors. Rich ores and underpaid native labor were the magnets that drew governments into the nets of concessionaires and brought to the peoples of the earth world wars.

Henry George was a prophet. His vision reached afar. Indeed, he saw all this taking shape. In his work, *Protection or Free Trade*, he wrote:

> Protection . . . has always found an effective ally in those national prejudices and hatreds which are in part the cause and in part the result of the wars that have made the annals of mankind a record of bloodshed and devastation—prejudices and hatreds which have everywhere been the means by which the masses have been induced to use their own power for their own enslavement.

Where is the informed person who will now challenge this statement? Surely it is plain to those who have taken the trouble to study the matter that one of the chief reasons for the First World War was the growth of German industry and the inroads that she made into markets beyond the seas, which had been special preserves of British manufacturers. As for the Second World War, both Great Britain and the United States entered the fray because Hitler had decided to abolish the system of foreign loans and to adopt a trade policy of barter.

In *Progress and Poverty*, George deals with the question of the diversities in social development. He points out that the social feeling ceases to be a factor in uniting families and tribes when they become separated from one another. Under certain circumstances, differences in language, custom, tradition, and religion foster the worst defects of political nationalism. He says:

> . . . With these differences, prejudices grow, animosities spring up, contact easily produces quarrels, aggression begets aggression, and wrong kindles revenge. And so between these separate social aggregates arises the feeling of Ishmael

and the spirit of Cain, warfare becomes the chronic and seemingly natural relation of societies to each other, and the powers of men are expended in attack or defense, in mutual slaughter and mutual destruction of wealth, or in warlike preparations. How long this hostility persists, the protective tariffs bear witness. . . .

He saw clearly that "warfare is the negation of association."

Only a few Georgists know how great a prophet George really was. Nearly all that is now taking place in the investigations in Washington, regarding political and social crime, was foreseen by him; and there are passages in his works which describe accurately the present appalling conditions in our great cities. Is not the following, taken from *Progress and Poverty*, a fairly complete picture of what is recorded in the daily papers?

> The type of modern growth is the great city. Here are to be found the greatest wealth and the deepest poverty. And it is here that popular government has most clearly broken down. In all the great American cities there is today as clearly defined a ruling class as in the most aristocratic countries in the world. Its members carry wards in their pockets, make up the slates for nominating conventions, distribute offices as they bargain together, and—though they toil not, neither do they spin—wear the best of raiment and spend money lavishly. They are men of power, whose favor the ambitious must court and whose vengeance he must avoid. Who are these men? The wise, the good, the learned—men who have earned the confidence of their fellow-citizens by the purity of their lives, the splendor of their talents, their probity in public trusts, their deep study of the problems of government? No; they are gamblers, saloon keepers, pugilists, or worse, who have made a trade of controlling votes and of buying and selling offices and official acts. They stand to the government of these cities as the Praetorian Guards did to that of declining Rome. He who would wear the purple, fill the curule chair, or have the fasces carried before him, must go or send his messengers to their camps, give them donatives and make them promises. It is through these men that the rich corporations and powerful pecuniary interests can pack the Senate and the bench with their creatures. It is these men who make School Directors,

Supervisors, Assessors, members of the Legislature, Congressmen. Why, there are many election districts in the United
States in which a George Washington, a Benjamin Franklin
or a Thomas Jefferson could no more go to the lower house
of a State Legislature than under the Ancient Regime a base-
born peasant could become a Marshal of France. Their very
character would be an insuperable disqualification.

Those who follow closely the evidence given in these
investigations of political and social crime might say
that the above statement, made more than seventy
years ago, is somewhat mild. It may be true that Henry
George did not foresee the full extent of this shocking
debasement of the public mind. No one could have
conceived a condition so alarming that our magazines,
for the past two years, have lamented the fact that the
people generally in the country have lost all sense of
rectitude and indignant protest.

In an extraordinary review of Anna George de Mille's
life of her father, which appeared in *The Times Literary
Supplement* (June 29, 1951), the critic, with unusual
sympathy, lauds the author of *Progress and Poverty* in
terms such as are seldom bestowed on men of single-
minded purpose. He says:

> The legacy of this remarkable man was not his policy of
> hypothesis. They did not give him the greatest public funeral
> New York had ever known for that. "He was the innocentest
> man that ever I knew," said his faithful Irish servant; and
> the epithet is most apt in its Latinity. He was the conscious
> symptom, the public conscience, of his society's *malaise*. That
> he did not discover the proper solution—or even that he found
> a wrong, or inadequate, one—is beside the point. He was
> perhaps the last of the great humanists. They could be wrong
> about means times without number, yet render humanity a
> profound service because they kept pointing to the right
> ends. Henry George's critique was of the ends which western
> industrial society had set itself. About the means of achieving
> them he could afford to err. But two generations after his
> death, and three after his book's first appearance, few
> thinking men anywhere in the West will refuse him the palm
> of the prophet. In spite of our progress, the Lady Poverty

abides with us, but in a guise the more terrible because it is less material.

Was Henry George wrong? If he did not find the proper solution of our economic woe, who did? It is inconceivable that a critic of repute, who shows in his writing that he is a fairly intelligent student of affairs, should labor under the delusion that a solution of the disabilities and afflictions of men are matters that may be left to the discretion of politicians. For, if George's solution is not the right one, then it is to be inferred that the State will discover some means of rectifying the evils which beset us.

Some European States have, for the past four generations, since the end of the Napoleonic Wars, tried every expedient to ameliorate the economic condition of the masses. As Jacques and Robert Lacour-Gayet show succinctly in *De Platon à la Terreur*, there is not one new political trick attempted by the modern State that has not been repeated many times ever since the days of Pericles. There has been a change of labels for the measures, but no matter what high-sounding title has been given to the dodge, it has, in practice, proved to be a very old one.

It is well our critic admits that in spite of our progress, poverty is still with us. In this respect, he agrees with George. But unlike the subject of his review, he does not ask why there should be involuntary poverty, and this is strange because he admits it is prevalent "in a guise more terrible because it is less material." Yet, make-work schemes, bonuses and doles, as sops and poultices for economic ills, have been administered by the State, decade after decade since Coxey's army marched on Washington and the British Fabians infiltrated into the Liberal party.

Today, material poverty in the whole of Europe threatens not only to destroy the best in its culture, but to drive its people to desperate action. Here, in our country, a war scare was necessary to save us from a slump. Early in the spring of 1950, the prospects of a letdown in trade were so serious that the government resorted to one of the oldest dodges of distracting the people—that of starting a war. But war was never yet a cure for involuntary poverty, and the expense of the Korean conflict, in men and treasure, was so fearful that it was a thoroughly unpopular one.

No matter how deeply our critic appreciates the character and purpose of Henry George, his review reveals the sad fact that he has not understood the gospel set forth in *Progress and Poverty*. Students of fundamental economics are, by now, conversant with the extraordinary notions some of our academic economists have held regarding the proposals for abolishing involuntary poverty. But I doubt whether anyone has ever read such a hodgepodge of confused thinking as our critic reveals in the following statement:

> . . . The Physiocrats had demanded the single-tax, *l'impôt unique*, and Voltaire had lampooned them in *L'Homme à Quarante Écus*, in which he asked why the peasant-farmer-landlord should pay everyone's taxes, and the manufacturer, merchant, shopkeeper escape. The second point is more puzzling: the "single tax" was not even new at that time. During the last third of last century even outstanding British Conservatives had advocated a single tax on capital (though not only land) values, or property. America had started the ill-fated, and regularly evaded, Personal Property Tax. And Henry George's sole taxation of land values seemed likely to hit the poorer nations, peoples, and continents harder than the richer, since they would be less able to finance their needs from such a tax. Thirdly, George affirmed that his tax would stick on the landlords, and would not shift, whereas Shearman and many other followers or admirers of George's ideas wanted the tax because they declared it *would* be shifted from the payer at its first incidence to everybody else in proportion.

Suppose we examine this extraordinary rigmarole and try to find if it has any relation at all to the ideas expressed by George. It does not follow, because Vol-

taire did not understand the proposals of Quesnay, that
"the peasant-farmer-landlord should pay everyone's
taxes." There is nothing in the literature of the Physiocrats that I have seen which suggests such a purpose.

To abolish taxes upon farms and take the rent of the
land, apart from improvements, was not only a relief
for farmers, but a similar fiscal system instituted in
urban areas would be a blessing for those who lived
and worked there. To be rid of the imposition of taxes
upon wealth was not only good for the farmer but also
for the merchant and the artisan in the towns.

It is amusing to think that our critic is one with so
many academic economists in being in no better position
to understand the proposals of Quesnay than Voltaire
himself. Certainly no progress toward a just fiscal system
has been made by these critics which can be recorded
as a credit, but the poverty of their ideas seems to grow
apace.

However, the confusion becomes more mixed in the
second point, which our critic says is "more puzzling";
"the 'single tax' was not even new at that time." At
which time? When Quesnay announced his proposal, or
when George wrote *Progress and Poverty?*

The next sentence is still more baffling, although we
may gather from it that the date of its newness is to be
found somewhere about the time George was writing
his work. "During the last third of the last century
even outstanding British Conservatives had advocated a
single tax on capital (though not only land) values, or
property."

It is news to me to learn of this. I should like to know
what authority there is for making such a statement.
When the Land Values Movement gathered strength
enough to force the Liberal party to make it one of the
chief reforms in its program, I became a candidate for a
county division. So far as I know, I was one of the first
to advocate a tax on the capital value of land from the
political platform.

True, the leagues for the taxation of land values, in England and Scotland, adopted the policy of Henry George shortly after his visit to Great Britain and Ireland. But in national politics, no one that I know of had made it a party question since the days of Richard Cobden when, in his speech at Derby, he demanded the taxation of land values for revenue to enable the government to abolish the breakfast-table duties.

In London, 1845, he said:

> I warn [the landlords] against ripping up the subject of taxation. If they want another league at the death of this one [the Anti-Corn Law League], then let them force the middle and industrious classes to understand how they have been cheated, robbed and bamboozled upon the subject of taxation.

From that time until the war began in 1914, the outstanding British Conservatives, as a political body, were bitterly opposed to such a measure.

It is difficult to unravel the tangle of notions referred to by our critic in the last sentence I have quoted. Does he mean a single tax on the value of capital? And what does he understand as capital? All the factories, shops and residences; all the tools, machines and furniture of all the buildings in the land? Or does he mean the capital value of the land, apart from improvements? The two last words of the sentence—"or property"—lead one to imagine that the single tax was not to fall on the value of land but on the wealth—property—that was produced from it by labor and capital.

In the fourth point, the critic refers to the confusion which "arose from the outset between the real whole-hogging single-taxers who would have taxed land and land alone . . . and those . . . who merely looked for, and found, an additional source of revenue by clapping a tax on the secular increment of land values."

The confusion is in the mind of the critic. No one suggested a tax on land. The tax was to fall on the value of it, and the Budget of 1909 called for a revaluation

of the land of England and Wales, and that was why
the bill was rejected by the House of Lords.

For fifty years a doubt has been lurking in my mind
as to the value of the knowledge of George's works his
critics have revealed in their strictures. Many of their
references indicate that they have either misread *Progress
and Poverty* or that they have merely learned from some
academic economist what he thinks about George's
ideas. I have never debated with an opponent, either
Socialist or Tory, who revealed a scintilla of evidence
that he was familiar with the books. And I may say
that I have seldom met even a single taxer who has read
A Perplexed Philosopher. All true Georgists that I have
known have considered that this critique of Herbert
Spencer's work on Justice was indispensable in the great
structure of fundamentals that George built up.

For those who consider the theories of Henry George
are out of date, and not applicable to the conditions
which exist, I would remind them that it is possible
to take whole sections from his books, which might
have been written this morning by an impartial observer.

As for the critic of Anna George de Mille's work, he
reveals in the following objection the cloven hoof of
the bureaucrat:

> . . . Fifth and lastly, George's book was in fundamental oppo-
> sition to all collectivisms, because its policy, devised merely
> as a means and not as an end, was to circumvent, not strength-
> en, the hand of the State on the individual citizen. It is odd
> that both George and the collectivists made the same error.
> Both based their policies on the old labour theory of value,
> whereas in an increasingly industrialized—and therefore
> capitalized—world, *the social utility theory of value alone can
> be safely employed as a measuring rod of reward, purposive planning,
> and efficacy of social policy.* . . . (italics mine)

These are mere phrases. And it is very difficult indeed
to learn from them just what the critic intends us to
know. It is true that George's book advocates a policy,
which is in opposition to collectivism, and that the

taking of rent and abolishing all taxes on wealth would weaken the hand of the State. But he says that "both George and the collectivists have made the same error."

This does not make sense. Surely the hand of the State is stronger and heavier today in all the principal nations than it has been since the days of imperial Rome; and collectivists are responsible for the growth of its power. He says George and the collectivists based their policies on the old labor theory of value. Does he mean "surplus value," as expounded by Marx? Surely he cannot mean that the full value of his product should be the reward of the laborer, as advocated by Henry George.

If this is not mixing theories that cannot possibly blend, I should like to know what it is. But the critic reveals his utter inability to clarify the matter when he says that "the social utility theory of value alone can be safely employed as a measuring rod of reward." Does he know any department of any State that has devised a method of ascertaining how value can be determined by the social utility theory? Is he oblivious to what is now taking place in Great Britain and this country, where men who are attempting to regulate the prices of commodities and the wages of labor, to say nothing of the return to capital, are thimblerigging the business morning, noon and night, and do not know what emergencies they will have to meet next week?

Now George, in *A Perplexed Philosopher*, describes accurately the very condition that exists in Britain and the United States:

> The truth is that customs, taxes, and improvement taxes, and income taxes, and taxes on business and occupations and on legacies and successions, are morally and economically no better than highway robbery or burglary, all the more disastrous and demoralizing because practised by the state. There is no necessity for them. The seeming necessity arises only from the failure of the state to take its own natural and adequate source of revenue—a failure which entails a long

train of evils of another kind by stimulating a forestalling and monopolization of land which creates an artificial scarcity of the primary element of life and labor, so that in the midst of illimitable natural resources the opportunity to work has come to be looked on as a boon. . . .

A financial and commercial journal of repute, in an article upon "The Tax Load," said: "We are in the gravest danger of being taxed into a depression that will cause irreparable chaos."

Would our critic say the "needs" of our State justify the fiscal robbery which grows by what it feeds on?

How long are we to tolerate this impertinent imposition of critics who write about George but do not take the trouble to read in *Progress and Poverty* the warning given about the necessity of understanding the meaning of economic terms? One of the chief features of George's work is his clear analysis of the meaning of the terms he uses: namely, land, labor, capital, wealth, rent, wages, and interest. No one, so far, has succeeded in controverting his definitions of these terms.

That a tax on land values might hit the poorer nations, peoples and continents harder than the richer, because they would be less able to finance their needs from such a tax indicates clearly to me that our critic should read *Progress and Poverty* once more, and strive earnestly to understand George's proposals. For here he implies that the expenditures of government under the system of the taxation of wealth are necessary.

I maintain there is not a government in Europe or America that could not manage its civil administration upon a third of what it now spends. The costliest "service" the taxpayers are called upon to maintain is that of the bureaucracy. Add to this the phenomenal waste of money that is thrown away upon the armed services, and it may easily be reckoned that the tax upon the value of land should be sufficient to pay the expenses of a country governed by honest men who have the taxpayers' interests at heart.

I could give many examples of what takes place in the departments in Washington and in most of the States concerning the waste of money, that goes on year after year. Here are two: A civil servant told me that at the end of World War II, in her department the majority of the staff had nothing to do but work out crossword puzzles, solve anagrams, and play the races on paper. The other instance was given me by an intimate friend who was made chairman of a State commission. After he had been in office for a month, he was appalled at the number of people in his department who had little or nothing to do. Within a year or so, he had cut the staff to about half and, being a shrewd judge of what people were capable of doing, he was not much surprised to find the work was being done more efficiently.

But Roosevelt's Civilian Conservation Corps beat all records for wasting the taxpayers' money. At one camp I visited, a corporal told me that two years' work on a road up a mountain went for nothing and that the old mule path, there before they attempted to make the road, was much safer for a motor car.

The so-called "needs" of revenue for spendthrift governments are now a byword. During the war a southern senator declared that "there must be some waste." Waste is still in progress, and the poverty of senatorial notions of how to stop it increases week by week. Indeed, the present tax burden threatens to put the producers of wealth out of their blue jeans into bottomless barrels, to hide their nudity.

The next point made by our critic is about the possibility of shifting a tax upon land value. How prices can rise in a falling market is a conundrum that has never been answered by those who believe landlords could shift the tax. I was told by the contractor of one of the largest estates in London that if a tax on land values were imposed, he would not know where to find the capital (tools) to set men to work to tear the ancient buildings down and erect modern ones. Over a large area, in that estate, there were streets of houses on lease which had been put up a hundred years previously. If the tax on land values could have been shifted, it would have been passed on to the tenant by the landlord or the lessees, and there would have been no reason whatever for the outcry which was raised by London landlords, when in 1909, the government introduced a bill calling for the revaluation of the land of England and imposed a small tax on the capital value. No one knows better than the landlord himself that, under such a system, he would be unable to shift the tax.

Landlords, then, would be in competition to find land users, and speculative value would come to an end. Two landlords for one land user would be the order of the day. And I might point out here that our critic should look up the speeches of Richard Cobden, delivered in the House and in the country, and try to understand what he meant when he told the Commons that the wage question was so simple that a child could understand it: two men for one job, low wage; two jobs for one man, high wage.

But legitimate competition is anathema to a sentimental Liberal, and the wonder of it is that so many of them imagine that they are free-traders. I remember addressing a meeting in London many years ago when I told the audience that they should consider that all men were land animals and could not live without land. A heckler in the audience shouted out, "What, all men?" For a moment I was stumped, and then an inspiration came to me and I retorted, "All men but Fabians and Marxists." I was amazed when the gentleman applauded loudly and gave me a cheer.

How strange it is that George's object explicitly set down is so seldom referred to by his critics. He says, the object is justice; the means, taxation. He saw the great injustice in the monopolization of land and its

resources and that it was the chief cause of involuntary
poverty. It was to remove this injustice that he began
to study the age-long problem and find a solution for
it. Hence, the pronouncement he made in *Progress and
Poverty* to abolish taxes upon wealth and take rent,
which belongs to the community, because land values
are created by its presence. Land is the source of all
their needs. All food, fuel, clothing and shelter are
produced from it by labor with the aid of capital.

Perhaps in this, George struck at the root of the
problem better than he knew. Although in the controversy with Herbert Spencer, as it is described so power-
fully in *A Perplexed Philosopher*, he touched the fountain
source of justice, I doubt whether he realized that he
was girding himself with the sword of Jesus of Nazareth.
When the Galilean presented himself to the Baptist at
Jordan, John said, "I ought to be baptized by thee, and
comest thou to me?

"And Jesus answering, said to him: Suffer it to be so
now. For so it becometh us to fulfil all justice. . . ."

The mission of Jesus was to establish God's justice
upon earth. For he was the seer who discovered the
purpose of his Father. When he said, "I will utter things
which have been kept secret from the foundation of
the world," he had divined the goodness of his Father
in giving the earth to *all* men for their sustenance. And
that, to him, was marked clearly in the distinction
between what was created and what was produced. He
knew from the Torah that property was wealth and
belonged to the producer. But that which was created—
the source from which food, fuel, clothing and shelter
were produced—was for all the children of God.

The great injunction of Jesus, the eternal imperative,
was: "Seek ye first the kingdom and its justice, and all
these things shall be added unto you." Perhaps it was
this, the first principle of the gospel, which inspired
Henry George.

Who can read the chapter entitled "The Central Truth," in *Progress and Poverty*, and not realize the deeply religious note that is sounded in it? It is without creed, cult, race, or color, and embraces all the peoples of the world. The tone is elevated, and the crescendo rises to poetic heights. The marvel of it is that all churches were not stirred by it.

Now that the world is in sore travail and millions in Europe and Asia cry for food and raiment, the appeal that George makes is more relevant to the conditions of the people than ever it was. Here, the whole structure is artificial. We are borne up on the waves of inflation, and the industrial wheels are kept spinning in making the munitions of war. But when the waves recede, what will happen in this land cannot bear thinking about.

We have had one experience of a depression, but unfortunately the lesson of it was not learned. Today a generation, which knows little or nothing of its afflictions, is carrying the burden of it. Although the mass of our people are employed, they live from hand to mouth. Mere nominal wage seems to satisfy the workers. But few understand how the value of the dollar has shrunk rapidly in the past two years. And, yet, the cry of the politicians is for more and more taxation to fill the maws of the spending departments. In this respect, our Congress out-Herods Herod in its greed for the revenue of the producers.

So it is with us as it has been with all civilizations in their decline. "Whom the gods destroy, they first make mad." The old saying, "*Quos Deus vult perdere prius dementat,*" should be emblazoned on every house of legislature in the land.

Henry George warned us of what would happen if we did not seek the kingdom. *Progress and Poverty* is the only book written by a layman of the west in which it is foretold, with a clarity that an intelligent student might understand, that the political and economic injustice of men would wreck their States.

George knew all the tricks and dodges of the palliatives politicians would prescribe for economic ills. And he realized that there was no hope coming from them for reconstruction, that generation after generation only political tinkers would be found to solder the widening seams in the rotten fabric of the State.

Nothing less than justice would satisfy George, and he knew that there could be no liberty without it. It is best to remind single taxers of the high ideals of George's gospel. There is far more in it than the matter of the means: taxation. It is the object that should always be kept in the forefront of the mission of Georgists:

> In our time, as in times before, creep on the insidious forces that, producing inequality, destroy Liberty. On the horizon the clouds begin to lower. Liberty calls to us again. We must follow her further; we must trust her fully. Either we must wholly accept her or she will not stay. It is not enough that men should vote; it is not enough that they should be theoretically equal before the law. They must have liberty to avail themselves of the opportunities and means of life; they must stand on equal terms with reference to the bounty of nature. Either this, or Liberty withdraws her light! Either this, or darkness comes on, and the very forces that progress has evolved turn to powers that work destruction. This is the universal law. This is the lesson of the centuries. Unless its foundations be laid in justice the social structure cannot stand.

Unerringly he divined that civilizations based upon injustice cannot continue. Indeed, he said that the eternal laws of the universe forbid it. A generation before Oswald Spengler wrote *The Decline of the West*, George prophesied our fate, if we neglected the duty imposed upon us by the great imperative of Jesus. What he asked for was:

> Something grander than Benevolence, something more august than Charity—it is justice herself that demands us to right this wrong. Justice that will not be denied; that cannot be put off—justice that with the scales carries the sword.

There is more true religion expressed in the gospel of Henry George than we hear from the pulpits of our land. And it was his faith in a beneficent Creator that gave him the courage to devote himself solely to the mission of ridding the earth of economic injustice and restoring the boon of equality of opportunity to all men.

INDEX

225

Ranke, Leopold von, 18, 24
Ravaillac, François, 87
Religion and the Rise of Western Culture, 37
Renan, Ernest, 6
Republic, The, 32
Rhodes, Cecil, 89
Richard I, 48-49, 191
Richard II, 42
Richard de Bury, 113-14
Robertson, John, 66
Robespierre, Maximilien, 118
Rogers, J. E. Thorold, 197
Roosevelt, Franklin D., 103, 175, 218
Royal Library, 80
Rule Britannia, 125
Russell, Bertrand (Lord), 47, 190-92

Sancta Clara, 99
Sandburg, Carl, 134
Savile, George, 85, 90
Schrödinger, Erwin, 14-15
Science and Humanism, 15
Scott, Sir Walter, 129
Seneca, 109
Shakespeare, William, 4, 43
Shaw, George Bernard, 189
Shearman, Thomas G., 212
Shelley, Percy Bysshe, 3, 76, 127, 130, 132
Shorthouse, John Henry, 98
Shrewsbury, Duke of, 44
Smith, Adam, 85, 89, 121
Socialism, 13, 21-22, 55, 146, 149, 154-58, 161, 164, 185-90, 206
Socrates, 12, 32, 35, 123, 201
Somers, Lord, 44, 85
Soule, George, 169, 172
Spencer, Herbert, 22, 36, 188, 215, 220
Spengler, Oswald, 9-12, 14-15, 46, 222
Stalin, Joseph, 18, 59, 186
Steffens, Lincoln, 165
Stephenson, George, 1
Stirling, J. H., 60
Suffield, Lord, 130
Swift, Jonathan, 44

Taylor, Bayard, 65-69, 76
Taylor, John, 173, 202
The Human Situation, 53, 123-24
"The New Learning," 116-17
Thomas, Norman, 169
Thomson, James, 125
Tilley, Dr. Arthur A., 108-09, 113-15
Tocqueville, Alexis de, 91, 101, 138
Toynbee, Arnold, 104
Trench, Archbishop, 203-04
Trevelyan, George, 3
Trotsky, Leon, 181, 186
Tucker, St. George, 202
Tugwell, Rexford, 169, 172
Turgot, Anne Robert Jacques, 121
Tyler, Wat, 126
Tyndall, John, 188

Universal Law(s), 62-64

Villiers, Charles P., 131
Virgil, 109, 111
Vollmar, George von, 153
Voltaire, 212-13

Wagner, Adolph, 23
Walsh, Gerald, 110
Ward, Wilfred, 79
Warham, Archbishop, 115
Washington, George, 95
Watt, James, 1, 196
Weaver, Richard M., 53-56
Webb, Sidney, 154, 189
Wellesley, Richard, 100
Wells, H. G., 189
Whitfield, J. H., 19
Whitney, Eli, 1
William III, 87
William of Orange, 190
Williams, Francis, 157
Wiseman, Cardinal, 79
Wordsworth, William, 127-28
Wright, Benjamin F., 203